The Syrian Arab Republic

The Middle East Confrontation States

THE SYRIAN ARAB REPUBLIC

A Handbook

Edited by

ANNE SINAI and ALLEN POLLACK

American Academic Association for Peace in the Middle East

New York

Main entry under title:
The Syrian Arab Republic: A Handbook.
(The Middle East confrontation states)
1. Syria. I. Sinai, Anne. II. Pollack, Allen, III. Series.
DS93.S86   956.91

Library of Congress Catalog Number: 76-17657

ISBN: 0-917158-00-8

Printed in the United States of America
Composition by Topel Typographic Corp., New York City

Table of Contents

IV

SYRIAN-ARAB RELATIONS

V

SYRIA AND THE SOVIET UNION

VI

SYRIA AND ISRAEL

VII

SYRIA IN THE INTERNATIONAL COMMUNITY

VIII

SYRIAN VIEWS

IX

SYRIA: A POLITICAL DIRECTORY

7

X
APPENDICES

THE SYRIAN ARAB REPUBLIC

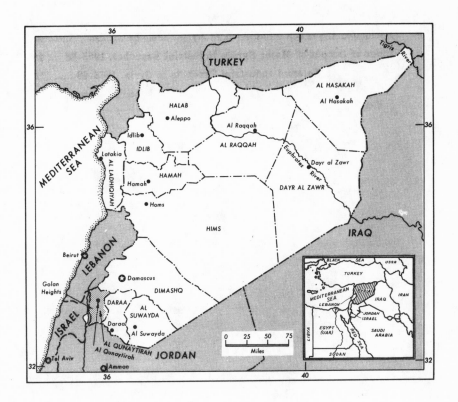

Source: *Area Handbook for Syria,* 1971, Second Edition.
(U.S.G.P.O. Washington, D.C. 20402)
Reprinted by permission.

Introduction

The Syrian Arab Republic is a new entity; the area known as Syria has been a center of many civilizations and cultures. Damascus was a seat of Christianity until the seventh century A.D., when the conquering armies of Islam made it the heart of a great empire. Western domination brought Western influence and ideas, inspiring in Syria a new kind of Arab nationalism deeply shaped by Islam and conceiving of the whole of the Middle East as forming one unitary Arab state. The conflict between this pan-Arab nationalism which transcends borders and denies the existence of separate nation-states, and Syria's modern need to define itself as a nation and to draw its many and diverse communities together into a cohesive social and cultural entity has been at the core of this country's many problems.

Syria, which had for centuries known no fixed borders and lacked a separate or distinctive political identity or a strong centralized government was constituted as an independent republic in 1946. For decades, its government was marked by instability, frequent purges and many changes in the political system. The fragility of its regimes brought about the intervention of the military in political life and culminated in Syria's decision to give up its independent existence in a merger with Egypt in 1958. The failure of this union led to the rise to power of the Ba'th (the Arab Renaissance) party and the Ba'th has ruled Syria ever since.

Ba'thist rule is based on an alliance of the military with the party organization and is exemplified in the person of President Hafez al-Assad, who is both an army officer and the head of the party. But the Ba'th's radical ideology, which has led to the nationalization of Syria's few industries and the redistribution of much of the arable land from the landowners to the peasants, has also added deep-seated problems to the Syrian polity. In a country where 90% of the population is Muslim, Ba'thist doctrine, formulated by Syrian Christian intellectuals, preaches secularism as well as radicalism and pan-Arabism. The secularist trend was reflected in the country's provisional constitution of 1969 and led to serious riots and disaffection. Amended in 1971, the constitution now includes the provisions that the president of the republic must be a Muslim and that Islamic jurisprudence is a principal source of legislation. The constitution—like Syrian society—is thus an amalgam of modern secular tendencies, superficial radical reforms and conservative Islamic values and relationships.

President Assad, who rose to power via a coup in 1970, has given Syria its most continuous government in decades, but the regime's stability is overshadowed by the continued cleavages and tensions within Syrian society. Assad is a member of the 'Alawite community which, though Muslim, is not Sunni Muslim and also not, strictly speaking, *Arab*. Although he has made efforts to attach the various ethnic communities to his regime, he must still solve the problem of his acceptance by the Sunni Muslim majority and he has not yet overcome their dislike of the dominant position that the 'Alawites hold in the army and the government.

Assad's efforts to make his regime acceptable has been based primarily on hostility toward Israel, Syria's southern neighbor, which came into being only some two years after Syria itself became an independent entity, and which is the only non-Muslim state in the region. Syria's attitude toward Israel has produced three wars and constant bloodshed along the long common border it shares with that country. For Syria, these wars have resulted in defeat and dislocation. The war of October 1973, for example, led to heavy casualties and the loss of additional territory to that lost in the war of 1967, yet Ba'thist pan-Arabism and the national xenophobia have contributed to the persistence of this country's war psychosis. What Syria could not achieve on the battlefield has been continued in the field of diplomacy and at U.N. forums. As it has often reminded its brother Arab states, it adheres to the principles of the Khartoum resolution of 1967: no peace with Israel, no negotiations with Israel, no recognition of Israel. The war against Zionism is inscribed in the preamble of the Syrian constitution and is an integral part of it.

Syria's position in the Arab world, in which it has struggled to gain legitimacy, has been closely linked to its domestic politics. Its ideology, which advocates the overthrow of existing Arab regimes—through subversion if need be—has not sat well with the existing Arab leaders. A weak and passive partner in inter-Arab politics for twenty years, Syria began to challenge Egypt's position as a center of radical politics in the 1960s. It was not until the early 1970s that President Assad succeeded in winning for Syria an increasingly important position in inter-Arab relations.

He has achieved this goal through his championship of the Palestinian organizations, not alone in the struggle against Israel but also in order to wrest ascendancy from Egypt. He has also managed to cement relations with Jordan, ending, however temporarily, a state of hostility that existed (between periods of wartime cooperation against Israel) for some thirty years. Syria's quarrel with Iraq over the Euphrates waters—essential to both countries' agriculture—remains unsettled but Assad's intervention in the Lebanese civil war (Syria still thinks of Lebanon as a part of Syria, as it was in the days of the Ottoman Empire) has greatly enhanced his position. Together with his stance of seeming "moderation" there, it has offered him a role as the possible leader of the northern tier of Arab states—the Fertile Crescent.

To bolster its regime, the Ba'th introduced the Soviet Union and the Communist bloc countries into Syria—a policy which Assad has continued and which has delivered to Syria massive quantities of sophisticated arms, Soviet technicians and Soviet economic assistance. Syria-Soviet relations are not free from tensions but the post-1970 crisis in Soviet-Egyptian relations has made that state extremely valuable to the Soviet Union as its only more or less reliable client in the Middle East.

Although, after the war of 1973, Syria made overtures to the United States—and the United States made overtures to Syria—it still continues to look mainly to the Soviet Union for its military and political support.

The Syrian Arab Republic may wish to play a leading role in the Arab world but it has few real assets. Its present policies, however, though they appear to be successful, are unlikely to help Syria realize its extravagant ambitions or to safeguard the country from serious military and political dangers in the future.

I

Syria, Past and Present

Syria Under Islamic and Ottoman Rule

From earliest times, the area known as Syria was populated by successive waves of Semitic peoples. The Hittites, the Egyptians, the Persians, the Macedonian Greeks, the Romans and the Byzantines have also left their imprint on this area, as have all the nomadic tribes wandering across the Middle East. Damascus may be the oldest capital city in the world. The town of Aleppo may be even older.

In A.D. 632, some six years after the death of the Prophet Muhammad, the conquering armies of the newly-created power of Islam reached through Palestine toward Syria. In Syria, the various populations who shared a Semitic language and culture and adhered in the main to the Monophysite faith[1] were hostile to their Greek-speaking Orthodox Byzantine rulers and therefore did little to oppose the invading Muslims, from whom they hoped to gain a greater measure of freedom. The Muslims defeated the Byzantine forces and in 636 virtually secured possession of all Syria. The Umayyad[2] dynasty which ruled Syria from 661-750 divided the area into four military districts (Damascus, Homs, Urdin [Jordan] and Palestine). Arabic became the official language and Syria itself became the heart of a great Muslim empire.

The new order in Syria, which represented the domination of a military caste of Muslim Arab warriors governing a non-Muslim, non-Arab subject people who had to pay tribute to the regime, changed gradually as Islam spread among the people. In theory, conversion to Islam meant, for the non-Arab converts (*Mawla,* pl. *Mawali*) full social and economic equality with the ruling caste, but in practice it was not enough to be a *Muslim*—one had to be an *Arab* as well. Their enforced inferiority created general discontent among the *Mawali*. It expressed itself in an appeal to the universal character of Islam, taking the form of religious heresies which grew more and more widespread.

In A.D. 750, with the accession of the Abbasid[3] dynasty, the center of the empire was transferred to Iraq while Syria became a mere province of that empire. In the ninth century, Syria became the object of dispute between Egypt

1. Monophysite doctrine believes that Christ has only one, divine, nature while the Orthodox believe that Christ has a double nature, divine and human. The Ethiopian, Armenian, Coptic and Syrian Jacobite Churches are Monophysite.

2. The House of Umayya was a branch of the House of Quraysh—Mecca's pre-Islamic keepers of the sanctuary and the mediators between groups of tribes. The Prophet Muhammad belonged to another branch of the House of Quraysh.

3. A branch of the House of Hashim, descended from the Prophet's uncle, which wrested the empire from the Umayyads.

and Baghdad. Reconquered by the Byzantines in the late tenth century, northern Syria became part of the Byzantine empire while the rest of the country remained in the hands of the Fatimid[4] dynasty enthroned in Egypt. In 1075, Damascus fell to the Seljuk Turks, but their rule soon disintegrated into a number of emirates. Seljuk princes ruled in Aleppo and Damascus, a local dynasty held Tripoli and Egypt controlled most of the littoral in the south.

This political fragmentation contributed to the success of the First Crusade, when Antioch and Jerusalem came under Christian rule. The Crusaders organized four feudal states: Edessa, Antioch, Tripoli and Jerusalem. Only the disintegration of Saladin's empire, after his death, into a number of separate principalities made it possible for the Crusaders to maintain their increasingly precarious hold on the coastal areas of Syria. This foothold was lost with the emergence, in Egypt, of the Mameluk[5] Sultanate.

Mameluk rule in Syria lasted until 1517 and was largely a time of slow decline, warfare, periodic famines and many outbreaks of the plague. The Mameluks ruled a loosely defined protectorate, subject to the growing power of the Ottoman Turks. In 1516 the Ottomans won Syria at the decisive battle of Marj Dabik, north of Aleppo and, a year later, conquered Egypt.

Ottoman rule brought only a temporary improvement in the condition of Syria, which was now divided into the three provinces *(vilayet)* of Damascus, Beirut and Aleppo. The Turkish pashas administered only the important towns and their immediate neighborhoods directly. In other areas of Syria, the older elements—Bedouin, emirs, Turcoman chiefs, etc.—were left to do much as they pleased, provided the regular tribute was paid. In time, as Constantinople's rule weakened, the pashas obtained greater freedom of action. Ahmed Jazzar, Pasha of Acre, for example, virtually ruled Syria as an independent monarch from 1785-1805.

Early in the nineteenth century, the Ottoman Sultan Mahmud II promised to give Syria to the Pasha of Egypt, Muhammad Ali, in return for Muhammad Ali's help during the Greek War of Independence. When the Sultan did not fulfill his promise, Egyptian troops invaded Syria and Muhammad Ali's son, Ibrahim Pasha, became Syria's ruler. He gave Syria a centralized government strong enough to hold the various separatist tendencies in check and to impose a regular, if burdensome, system of taxation. The Syrian landowners were opposed to his efforts to limit their social and political domination and the peasantry disliked the conscription, forced labor and heavy taxation he imposed. A revolt broke out in 1840. The Great Powers intervened on behalf of the Sultan, who was at war with Egypt, and Muhammad Ali was forced to renounce his claim to Syria.

Ibrahim Pasha had encouraged trade with the West and also the Western

4. This dynasty came to power by conquering the Maghreb and then Egypt.
5. A military regime composed of Turks and later of Circassians.

powers' efforts to protect the Christian minorities in Syria and to found missions and cultural and educational institutions in the area. The predominant Western influence was that of France, which established special ties with the Maronite community. French Jesuits opened schools in Syria in 1831 and in 1875 founded their university at Beirut. The American Presbyterian Mission in Beirut introduced a printing press and founded the Syrian Protestant College (later renamed the American University of Beirut). Syria also benefited from the reform movement within the Ottoman Empire itself. The semi-independent pashas were swept away, the administration was entrusted to salaried officials of the central government, some attempt was made to create schools and colleges and much was done to deprive the landowning classes of their feudal privileges—although their social and economic predominance was left unchallenged.

In the late nineteenth century there was a revival of Arabic literature. This was an important factor in the growth of the Arab nationalism of the twentieth century.

Syria Under the French Mandate

The area known as Syria was part of the Ottoman Empire from 1517 to the end of World War I. In the nineteenth century, as Ottoman power declined, Western influence began to spread. There was economic and cultural penetration—soon followed by political and military intervention. Western influence—and intervention—gave birth to Western ideas. The most potent of these, in Syria as in the Arab world as a whole, was that of nationalism. But Arab nationalism did not view Syria or any other Arab state as an independent territorial entity: Syria had to be a part of an independent Arab world. Arab nationalism emerged in Syria on the eve of World War I, with the creation of semi-secret societies which demanded autonomy, decentralization and increased participation in Ottoman governmental institutions. This latter demand quickly encountered the opposition of the "Young Turks" who had overthrown the old regime in Constantinople in 1908. The active nationalists in Syria were few in number, had very little political influence and were fragmented into many factions but when the Ottoman Empire joined Germany and Austro-Hungary in World War I new opportunities opened up for them.

The British had contacted Sharif Hussein of Mecca (with whom the Syrian nationalists had also been in touch) and promised him their support for the creation of an Arab state which would also include Syria—with the reservation (in keeping with the secret Sykes-Picot Agreement of 1916)[6] that the western coast lands would be set aside for a future French administration. The "Arab Revolt" in Hejaz in 1916 did not lead to an uprising in Syria but when, in 1918,

6. See p. 160.

the Ottoman Empire collapsed and Syria was conquered by the Allies, Arab troops commanded by the Emir Feisal, son of Sharif Hussein, entered Damascus to be greeted with wild enthusiasm by the population. In Damascus, the Emir Feisal set up an Arab government and gradually took over the administration, but Syria's political status remained unclear.

In keeping with the promises made in the McMahon-Hussein[7] correspondence, Britain supported the establishment of an Arab state. In the Arab view, this state was to spread over Palestine as well as other areas.[8] When Britain demurred, the Arabs pointed to the Balfour Declaration and the Sykes-Picot Agreement as evidence of British bad faith. In addition, Britain's support of an independent Arab state angered the French, who found it in direct conflict with the Sykes-Picot Agreement, which had delineated the interior of Syria as a French "area of influence" while leaving the coastal areas under direct French administration. The Syrians themselves, while demanding complete independence, nevertheless had many different notions about the future of Syria and these notions were colored by religious and community rivalries and fears, as the King-Crane Commission[9] of 1919 discovered. The Commission's general impression was that if independence was not to be gained a U.S. mandate was. generally preferred (on the grounds that the Americans were "very rich" and not tainted by colonialism) and that Great Britain was the next choice. Palestine, the *'ulama*[10] insisted must be under Muslim control. A French mandate was widely opposed; only the Greek Catholics preferred France as the mandatory power in Syria. The other Christian sects, fearing that an independent Muslim Arab government would endanger their rights, were mainly in favor of a British mandate. The Syrian nationalists were only in agreement on one issue: they persisted in regarding Lebanon and Palestine as integral parts of Syria. (TransJordan had also been regarded by the nationalists as part of Syria but Britain had given the territory of Palestine east of the Jordan River to Feisal's brother, the Emir Abdallah ibn Hussein, in 1922.)

Article XXII of the League of Nations Covenant did not favor the immediate independence of any detached part of Turkey. Syrian nationalists voiced their opposition to this Article by calling, at the General Syrian Congress of 1919, for the creation of an Arab Government in Iraq without customs restrictions or strictly defined borders between Iraq and Syria. They also demanded a common educational system "to prepare the Arab people for unity as soon as possible."

As the French became more entrenched on the coast the antagonism of the nationalists intensified, erupting in frequent clashes. The Syrian Congress of

7. See. p. 158.

8. Palestine had not, nevertheless, been included in the plans projected for the Arabs by the Sykes-Picot agreement and, although the language is vague, had not been included in the projected Arab state promised by McMahon to Hussein.

9. See. p. 157.

10. The Muslim religious leaders.

1920 proclaimed Feisal King of Syria (without defining Syria's borders but implying the inclusion of what is at present Lebanon and what was then British Mandatory Palestine). Britain and France refused to recognize this proclamation. The San Remo Conference of April 1920 conferred the Mandate for Syria upon France. More armed clashes followed. French troops entered Damascus on July 25, 1920 and overthrew Feisal.

From the very onset, the Syrians—and the Sunni Muslim Arab majority in particular—hated the French rule which had been imposed on them. In an effort to weaken this opposition, the French based their administration upon the support of ethnic and religious minorities and especially on the Christians of Mount Lebanon. They established a state of "Greater Lebanon" and added the Muslim majority districts in the north and south and also the city of Beirut to create an area in which the Christians formed the majority and as a result Syria lost areas of vital importance to her economic viability. The French also divided the rest of Syria into separate administrative units, thus emphasizing separatist minority interests. The Lataqia region, chiefly inhabited by 'Alawites, became a separate administrative unit, as did Jabal Druze and the district of Alexandretta (which had a large Turkish minority). The states of Aleppo and Damascus were created, linked in a federation and then united into the "State of Syria" in 1924-5, while the relative autonomy of the three other regions continued.

The various Syrian states were given constitutions and councils but the real authority rested with the French High Commissioner in Beirut. The French Mandatory government improved public security and administration but it always remained the hated foreign ruler. A local uprising in Jabal Druze in 1925 quickly became a national uprising. The French were unable to quell it until 1927.

France now agreed to grant Syria a form of nominal independence based on a treaty granting the mandatory power various special privileges and the right to maintain troops and bases. Lebanon was declared a republic in May 1926 and granted a constitution and parliamentary institutions, but only in 1928 did the French High Commissioner do away with military government in Syria and permit elections for a constituent assembly. The elections were won by the "National Bloc"—a coalition of several nationalist parties united only by their opposition to the French.

The National Bloc prepared a draft constitution which demanded, inter alia, the re-unification of what was termed "all Syria." The French rejected this demand and dissolved the Assembly in 1930. The High Commissioner proclaimed a constitution establishing a republican regime and providing for a Chamber of Deputies to be elected for a four-year term. The Chamber was also to élect a President of the Republic, with limited powers.

The National Bloc lost much of its strength in the elections which were held in 1932 but their members in the Chamber saw to it that all French proposals to replace the Mandate were squashed. The Chamber was dissolved in 1934, the tension in French-Syrian relations increased and riots broke out in 1936.

That year, the "Popular Front" government of French Socialist leader Leon Blum signed a Franco-Syrian treaty which promised that Syria would become independent within three years and could incorporate the territories of Jabal Druze and Lataqia (although these would still maintain a measure of autonomy). France was to equip and train an indigenous Syrian Army but would at the same time maintain troops and military bases in Syria. The treaty was quickly ratified by the newly elected Chamber, where the National Bloc regained its majority, but France then refused to ratify it.

Syria's search for a political settlement with France continued but the Syrian nationalists' opposition to the French marred the country's economic progress and also its political life. The nationalists were split into many opposing factions. Assassinations, separatist movements, anti-administration protests and clashes were ever-present in the 1930s.

When France fell to Hitler in June 1940, French officials in Syria remained loyal to the Vichy government and allowed Italians and Germans to penetrate into the area. Their growing domination led to a British invasion of Syria and Lebanon in June 1941. General Georges Catroux, the new French Governor, proclaimed the termination of the Mandate and the independence of Syria, but the French government was slow in transferring Syria to the Syrians and in re-establishing parliamentary institutions. Elections were held (after France finally succumbed to British and American pressure) in 1943. The National Bloc won the majority again and its leader, Shukri Quwwatli, was elected President of Syria.

The Soviet Union and the United States recognized Syria in 1944; Britain in 1945. The newly-created Arab League also gave the new republic its support. In January 1945, Syria announced the establishment of a national army, declared war on the "Axis" powers and consequently became one of the founding members of the U.N. The French shelled Damascus again (as in the riots of 1925) when anti-French riots broke out in May because of French reluctance to withdraw its troops. A British ultimatum forced a cease fire. The British and French then agreed to withdraw their troops by the end of the year—an agreement which did not satisfy the Syrian government, since its wording implied that a special, privileged status would still remain for France in Syria and Lebanon. Syria lodged a complaint with the U.N. Security Council on this issue. The Soviet Union vetoed a resolution calling for negotiations and a speedy withdrawal but this conflict was settled by mid-April 1946, when France withdrew all her garrisons.

Syria, 1946-1958

Syria had become an independent country, free of the hated French domination and free also to shape its own destiny. What path it would follow was, however, complicated by many diverse and often contradictory and antagonistic forces. As a member of the Arab world the newly created Syrian state joined the other Arab states in their war to exterminate the newly created state of Israel. Internally one of Syria's basic problems was its need to define its own nationhood.

It has been pointed out that "Syria" is a modern entity and a modern concept. The idea of Syria as a nation—as a separate entity—was first formulated in the second half of the nineteenth century by Syrian and Lebanese Christians. As members of non-Muslim communities in a Muslim world they had a privileged but inferior status. The idea of nationalism therefore meant, to them, that they could claim equal citizenship and status with Muslims in a modern nation-state. They were the first to propound the doctrine of secular nationalism; of a state in which the basis of identity was language and culture and not religion and community. The Lebanese Christians in particular played a very important role in the founding and development of Arabic literature and many Christians in Syria and Lebanon became the first leaders and intellectuals of the nationalist movements in the Arab world as a whole. To the Muslims on the other hand, secular nationalism—the idea of a self-contained Syrian state—was not as powerful an attraction as it was to the Christians. The Muslims regarded themselves as primarily members of the whole Islamic community; their loyalty belonged to Islam as a whole and therefore to pan-Arab nationalism which conceived of all the areas of the Arab world as forming one, unitary state. There was place for separate ethnic and cultural groups in this state, but, as in the days of the old caliphate, the state itself had to be Islamic and had to extend over the whole of the Arab world.

During their struggle against the French, certain groups had come to have vested interests in the French-created political unit called Syria. These vested interests were a strong force in prodding Syria's Muslim nationalists to call for Syria's unification and independence, but even these interests were not free of the dominant ideology of pan-Arab nationalism or of allegiance to their own particular community in the many internal divisions within the Syrian population. For in Syria, as in other areas of the Arab world, effective political loyalty was often still vested in traditional social or regional units. To the individual Syrian, loyalty to his family, religious community, tribe and locality was far more important than loyalty to a state. The extended patrilinear family still remains the basic unit of all Syrian society and family loyalty still transcends all other ties.[11]

11. See Article 44:1 of the Syrian Constitution, p. 170, which recognizes this concept.

Added to these factors was the diversity and fragmentation of Syrian society and the weakness of the political center. Sunni Muslims form the majority element in the country, but the formerly autonomous communities constitute some 40% of the population and have always tended to be suspicious and distrustful of the Sunni majority. In the 1940s and even to the mid-1960s the country's political and economic life was still dominated by a small, mostly Sunni elite whose members lived in Aleppo and Damascus. The Sunni land-lords had large estates which were worked by a heterodox peasantry. In general, the Sunni majority tended to regard the Christian and heterodox Muslim groups as "imperfect Arabs,"[12] an attitude that still affects the coun-try's minority groups today.

There was the need for Syria to define its political community and to integrate its minorities and this process was made all the more complicated by the attempted interference of other Arab states and the Western powers in Syrian affairs. The doctrine of pan-Arabism, the weakness of the new state's structure and the traditional orientations of Syria's regions and ethnic groups only made this outside interference all the easier.

A steady weakening of the political and social power of the old ruling class did, nevertheless, gradually take place in the late 1940s as younger, more radical groups appeared on the scene. This change was marked by three coups in 1949. The coups gave the military a new and decisive role in Syria's political life—and the military has remained a major factor in Syrian politics ever since.

The coups resulted in the military dictatorship of Adib Shishakli (1949-1954). He set up a state-organized single party and a parliament which gave urban, lower-middle class elements strong representation. Shishakli was over-thrown by his close associate, Akram al-Haurani, who joined forces with the small and relatively new and radical Ba'th Party (founded by Michel 'Aflaq and Salah-al-Din al-Bitar in 1940) to attain power. Once in power, Haurani founded his own Arab Socialist Party by organizing the peasants of the Homa district against their landlords. As a former fighter in al-Kaukji's[13] 1948 campaigns in Palestine he also had close ties with the army. To consolidate his position, he agreed to a merger of his Arab Socialist Party with the Ba'th.

The new, unified Ba'th Party formed a coalition with the Druze and several conservative groups and won 22 of the 142 seats in the Chamber in the comparatively free elections of 1954. A coalition of the Ba'th and the small Syrian Communist Party began moving Syria closer to the Soviet Union. The Nasser regime in Egypt, which had begun to pursue a more active pan-Arab policy, was however an equally strong contender for influence in Damascus.

12. See Albert Hourani, *Syria and Lebanon: A Political Essay* (Oxford University Press, 1971). pp. 127-128.

13. Fawzi al-Kaukji, a Syrian, led an Arab volunteer force into Palestine in January 1948 which took control of the northern Arab villages. His "Army of Deliverance" attacked Jewish settlements and mixed towns.

The Ba'th and Communist alliance drew its power from the support of the army. But the army contained both conservative and "radical" elements and the officers' corps was fragmented and split into numerous rival factions and despite frequent purges, a strong conservative element still remained in it. The Ba'thist officers were, at best, only loosely linked to the party and mainly through Haurani. This led to tension between the 'Aflaq and Haurani wings of the party and the Ba'th itself was of two minds on policy. It believed, on the one hand, in revolutionary preparation as a precondition to assuming power and on the other hand it was eager to seize power by a short cut. All these tensions led to the serious political crisis of 1957 and propelled the Ba'th and its army officer allies into Syria's union with Egypt in 1958.

The Union With Egypt

Syria in 1957-58 was on the verge of political disintegration, faced with the threat posed by the growing strength of its Communist Party, the strong pressure of its conservative groups and the open hostility of its Turkish and Iraqi neighbors. Rival army factions were on the verge of clashing. The only way to stop the creeping chaos appeared to be through a union with Egypt.

There were many other reasons for the Ba'th's decision. Egypt was Syria's ally in the Arab economic and propaganda war against Israel. Egypt had suffered defeat in the Sinai war of 1956 but it was a defeat that the radicals felt had made Nasser a heroic victim of imperialist attack. Nasser's charisma had great popular appeal in Syria. He had made Egypt a "progressive" Arab power and appeared to be a suitable partner in helping to achieve the Ba'thist dream of Arab unity. The army saw the union with Egypt as a way to halt its own suicidal factionalism and to preserve its paramount position in Syria's political life, and many other elements preferred a union with Egypt to complete disintegration.

The Ba'th and the army approached Nasser with the intention of discussing a federal union, but quickly acceded to his demand for 1) a merger of the political patterns in both parts of the new united state; 2) the dissolution of all the political parties in Syria; and 3) the termination of the Syrian army's role in politics.

The United Arab Republic (of Egypt and Syria) came into being in February 1958. To the Ba'th it was a first stage in the achievement of a radical unitary state in the whole Middle East. To Nasser it was the first stage in Egypt's gradual incorporation of Syria. The Syrian Ba'th was Nasser's first victim and he ruthlessly scattered and suppressed its leadership. Egyptian officers and officials soon came to be hated by the country as a whole and the steady erosion of Syrian support for the union destroyed it within three years. It was terminated by the army officers' coup of September 28, 1961.

The coup was carried out by two separate elements: rightists linked with the Syrian middle class and the conservative Arab regimes and a group which did not really want to break away from the union but only wished to reform it by imposing certain conditions on the Egyptians. The immediate effect of the failure of the union was to reopen the issue of Syria's national identity. It helped to give Syrians a new sense of their national distinctiveness and brought forward the new idea of the existence of a special and separate Syrian state.

The union with Egypt also had other important effects. It gave Syria its Agrarian Reform Law of September 1958 and its nationalization decrees of July 1961, which are still in effect. It had important consequences for the Ba'th party. Harassed by the UAR authorities, the Ba'thist rank and file came to resent the Ba'th leadership. Among the educated Ba'thist members there was a sense of disenchantment with the party's original ideology and a move toward greater extremism. Dissidents organized their own pro-Nasserite Ba'th party and the Haurani and 'Aflaq factions drew further apart.

But it was the Ba'thist army officers who had been hardest hit by the union. Many of them had been sent into virtual exile in Egypt and their hatred and bitterness was all the more intensified by the fact that they were in the main 'Alawites, (non-*Arab* Muslims and therefore not members of the Sunni Muslim elite).[14] While in Egypt, thirteen of them formed a secret group—"The Military Committee." They were opposed to the UAR authorities, to the party's veteran leaders (whom they blamed for their plight) and to the traditional Ba'thist military leaders and in particular to the high-ranking officers associated with Haurani. The Military Committee's leaders were three 'Alawite officers: Muhammad 'Umran, Salah J'did and Hafez al-Assad.

The Syrian Arab Republic

Following Syria's break—via the officers' coup—with Egypt, a new, temporary constitution was proclaimed in Damascus. Elections were held and a Constituent Assembly was elected but it lacked political stability and was too conservative to suit the radical elements in the army. It was overthrown in an officers' coup in March 1962, reinstated when the officers could not agree among themselves, had to cope with unrest in the cities as well as in the army and became only the more unstable.

A Ba'th coup took place in Iraq in February 1963. On March 8, 1963 the Syrian Ba'th and its army officer supporters staged a coup of their own. The Ba'thist strongman who emerged after several months of factional struggle was the Sunni general Amin al-Hafez, who let the Ba'th purge the army and government of pro-Nasserite elements. A Nasserite attempt to overthrow him failed.

The Ba'th now attempted to create a united front with its sister-regime in Iraq, but the Iraqi Ba'th regime was overthrown in November and with it went

14. See p. 62.

the Ba'th's last hopes for some form of renewed union with Egypt (this time in the shape of a tripartite federation to include Iraq). Egyptian-Syrian relations were not renewed until 1966, when both states signed a military pact. Formal diplomatic relations were only re-established in the spring of 1967.

Inside Syria, Hafez's Ba'th government proclaimed a new constitution and began to implement a policy of nationalizing banks and factories and distributing land to the peasants. Merchant and landowner riots and protest demonstrations were brutally put down.

But the Ba'th leadership had by this time split into two rival factions. One supported the party's founders, was more moderate on nationalization and supported Arab unity and a renewed future alliance with Egypt. The other, consisting of younger party leaders, many of them 'Alawites and Druzes, was more radical, advocated a speed-up in nationalization measures and was anti-Nasserite. This faction, known as the party's "military wing" had its greatest support among the officer's corps, in which minority groups—and 'Alawites in particular—predominate.

In 1965, the party's "moderate", "civilian" wing ousted the members of the rival "military" wing from their positions and began to carry out purges. The "military" wing staged a coup in February 1966 and arrested the old leadership. Among those put in prison were 'Aflaq, Bitar and General Amin al-Hafez.

The new leaders of Syria were two 'Alawite Ba'thist Generals: Salah J'did, who was supported by the "regional" (Syrian) Ba'th and Hafez Assad, Commander of the Air Force and Minister of Defense—and the two soon became rivals. Lacking a broad base, they allied themselves with the Syrian communists, who were granted representation in the government for the first time in Syria's history.

During 1966 there were widespread political purges. The regime gave the key positions in the army, the central government and local administration to its trusted supporters and gained control over the trade-unions and the students, farmers and women's associations. It claimed to have redistributed one third of the cultivated land to the peasants by 1967.

Syria now strengthened its ties with the Soviet Union[15] and tried to improve its relations with Egypt. In its efforts to gain legitimacy in the Arab world, its hostility toward Israel grew all the more extreme: the Syria-Israel border became an arena of violent clashes and constant tension—one of the decisive causes of the Arab-Israel war of 1967.

For Syria, the war resulted in the occupation of the Golan Heights by Israeli

15. From 1954 to 1970 Syria received over $580 million in arms and some $443 million in economic assistance from Soviet-bloc countries and was the seventh highest recipient of Soviet aid of all the underdeveloped countries (Department of State, Bureau of Intelligence and Research, *Communist States and Developing Countries Trade and Aid;* Washington, D.C., September 22, 1971).

forces, the Israeli army's swift advance to within 38 miles of Damascus and a residue of refugees from the Quneitra region who, though they could today be resettled in that area, still live in refugee camps in Damascus. Syria accepted a cease-fire but vowed, in the most extravagant and extremist terms, to renew the war with Israel. It did not participate in the Arab summit conference at Khartoum, rejected Security Council Resolution 242 of November 1967[16] and refused to cooperate with U.N. intermediary Gunnar Jarring and offered ready bases and arms for increased sabotage activities against Israel to the Palestinian organizations and to al Fatah in particular. However, it soon became clear that Syria intended to take this organization over. This task was assigned to a Palestinian officer in the Syrian army, Captain Yussuf Urabi, who promptly informed all the Fatah units that Arafat was dismissed and was promptly murdered by one of Arafat's agents. The Fatah-Syrian amity of 1966 ended with the imprisonment of the top Fatah leaders, including Arafat. Syria then created its own Palestinian group—al Sa'iqa—now the second largest of the organizations after al-Fatah. Palestine Liberation Army units and all other PLO groups in Syria have never been permitted to set up independent establishments and all their activities have always been strictly supervised and controlled.

Splits in the ruling Ba'th junta continued. In October 1968, its "nationalist" group led by General Hafez al-Assad gained the upper hand. The group's aim was to reduce Syria's dependence upon the Soviet Union, to improve relations with the other Arab states and to renew the war against Israel.

Assad and his "nationalists" began arresting the communists and making changes in the government. (Assad had virtually taken control of the government in February 1969 in a kind of semi-coup, but Syria's continued dependence on Soviet military and economic aid—and also Egyptian pressure—had forced him to accept a compromise and the continued participation of the "leftist" faction in the government.) The regime also tried to meddle in the relations between the Palestinian organizations and the governments of Lebanon and Jordan. (During the civil war in Jordan, in September 1970, Syrian forces actually marched into that country but were driven back.)

General Assad completed his takeover of the Syrian government in November 1970. His first step was to arrest all his opponents. A 173-member "People's Council" was convened in February 1971. The Council nominated Assad as President of the Republic. He was endorsed that same month in a plebiscite (in which he was the only candidate).

Assad's first move was to mend Syria's relations with the other Arab states, and especially with Egypt. He announced, in December 1970, that Syria would join a proposed Egyptian-Libyan-Sudanese Federation. In the summer of 1971 he sent emissaries to mediate between King Hussein of Jordan and the Palesti-

---

16. Syria accepted the Resolution in the French translation, i.e., "withdrawal . . . from *all* territories . . ."

nian organizations—an effort that did not meet with Jordanian approval—and Syria returned to its former anti-Jordanian attitude. Assad indicated however, that he would agree to the revival of the joint "Eastern Command" against Israel.[17]

Assad's efforts toward rapprochement with Egypt led to the two countries' coordinated attack on Israel in October 1973—an alliance that did not last for more than a matter of months. Despite his wariness of the Soviet tie, Soviet and communist bloc military and economic aid—and the Soviet presence in Syria—increased at a rapid pace.

Syria Today

President Assad has given Syria its most stable government in decades. He is also the first Syrian statesman in the modern era who appears to be succeeding in drawing the whole population together by striving to transcend communal and party differences.

The hard core of his support stems from the military—and in particular from the 'Alawite officers who occupy the senior positions in the army[18]—but Assad has also made efforts to appoint Sunni, Druze and Christian officers who are loyal to the regime to senior positions. As Commander-in-Chief he has worked to make the army the solid foundation for the regime, transcending communal affiliations. Under his guidance it has become the largest and the strongest military power in the Fertile Crescent.

The regime's link with the Ba'th party is another important source of its strength. The party apparatus reaches throughout the country, to even the most far-flung villages and its members are organized in a strict hierarchy. Party workers have been appointed to senior positions in the civil service and other branches of the administration. The Ba'th's control of the trade unions and the various other organizations extends its influence to all the members of these organizations and to their families.

The regime has raised the workers' living standards and, in the nationalized and public industrial plants, distributed 40% of the profits among the workers (the remainder is equally divided between industry and government). It has distributed expropriated lands among the *fellahin* (peasants) and set up agricultural cooperatives—although not without the necessity for certain coercive

17. See p. 154.

18. Assad's brother, Rif'at, is in command of an elite corps assigned to protect the regime's nerve centers.

measures. It has given itself the cast of democracy by holding referenda to approve important decisions.[19]

The army, the party organization, the secret police and the government's control of the media have all contributed to the regime's stability.

Assad's greatest prestige stems from his role in the war of October, 1973 which, though it involved the loss of Syrian territories, inflicted heavy casualties and severely damaged the economy, nevertheless enhanced his image as a pan-Arab leader. In his speeches, he called the war a *jihad*—a holy war against the infidel and Zionism, "the enemies of Islam." The Syrian army was termed the army of Allah, and its slogan was: *Death for the Glory of Allah, or Victory*. The war itself became known in the Arab world as the *War of Ramadan* (the Muslim Holy Month of Fasting)—a term inspired by Egypt. In this way, the leader of Syria emphasized the Islamic background of the Arab-Israel conflict and also acknowledged the importance of Islam in Syria. That he is extremely sensitive to the need to conciliate the *'ulama* and the religious sentiments of the Muslims of Syria was initially evidenced by his restoration of the presidential oath in June 1971. ("I swear by Allah Akhbar" replaced the former secular oath, "I swear on my honor and my faith".) In February 1973 (following serious riots), Assad also restored the paragraph in the Constitution establishing that the president must be a Muslim.

In his efforts to identify the broad section of the people with his regime, Assad has, since 1973, also attempted to conciliate the small group of Syrian businessmen and manufacturers and the middle classes by easing the former regime's economic policies and by encouraging private initiative, and his "open" and "fatherly" approach to the masses of the people appears to be helping to foster, in ethnically and communally divided Syria, a growing sense of nationhood.

The regime is not, however, without its difficulties, political and economic. In April 1975, the sixth regional (Syrian) Congress of the Ba'th—the highest forum of the Syrian Ba'th—gave radical elements opposed to what they regard as Assad's "soft" policy toward Israel the opportunity to record their opposition—and their strength—by challenging the "official" candidates to the various committees. Assad reacted to this upsurge of opposition by making significant changes in the Ba'th's power structure. Seven new members were elected—the newcomers are men who owe their power and careers to Assad— and some old members were dropped.

On its economic front, Syria enjoyed windfalls of aid from Arab sources in 1974 to compensate for the economic havoc caused by the October 1973 war. This aid totalled between $1 billion and $1.5 billion (compared with only $60

19. The March 1971 referendum approved Assad's election as president by 99% of the vote. The Syrian Constitution was approved in a referendum by 98% of the vote. Of the 186 seats in the Syrian parliament, the National Progressive Front, headed by Assad, won 140 seats, the Ba'th won 122 seats and the rest were won by non-Ba'th candidates in the May, 1973 elections.

million from all sources in 1973). Agricultural production experienced a boom. There was a sharp increase in revenues from oil and phosphates. (Oil, which had formed 15% of Syria's export income in 1973 amounted to some two-thirds of foreign revenue in 1974.)

Despite Soviet credits for purchases of arms and equipment, however, 1975 was estimated to show a balance-of-payments deficit of about $500 million, due mainly to expenditure on the armed forces (at a cost of $1 billion-$1.5 billion). The individual citizen has been hard hit; the cost of living rose over 50% in 1974 alone.

The image of a stable regime which Assad has presented to the world has also been somewhat flawed by his dispute with Iraq and Iraqi revelations of his determination to hunt out plots and crush opposition. The regime has, in addition, rooted out adherents of "The Arab Communist Organization" in a trial that ended in death sentences for five of its members on July 29, 1975. While wooing its members in various ways, it has nevertheless also persecuted the ultra-conservative Muslim Brotherhood, which has always been opposed to the supposedly "atheistic" nature of Ba'th doctrine and the prevalence of schismatic 'Alawite Muslims in the seats of power. There have been reports of conspiracies by officers and men who oppose the trend toward cooperation with the U.S. (which they profess to see in Assad's present policy) and there have been riots in Damascus and Aleppo, followed by clashes and exchanges of fire between the army and civilians.

Syria's rift with Egypt has widened in the past year. It has accused Egypt of behaving unilaterally without consulting its "wartime brother-in-arms" in signing the interim disengagement agreement with Israel and has belittled the value of the "small areas" that were being returned to Egypt, stressing the "lost Arab unity" this has entailed and reminding Egypt of the three Noes of the Khartoum (1967) Arab summit meeting: no peace with Israel; no negotiations with Israel; no recognition of Israel.

The dominant role Syria has played in the Lebanese civil war, on the other hand, has raised Assad's prestige immensely in the Arab world.

President Assad's external reputation has little to do with the serious internal problems his country must still confront. Perhaps the most realistic view of Syrian society today was provided by Dr. Razak Allah Hilan, writing in the official government party newspaper, *Al Ba'th,* on October 11, 1974:

> A year has passed since the sixth of October and what have we done in that year? Have we maintained the same spirit and fortified it with creative effort, that would serve as a burning torch to light the way for us, burn away the corruption, purge society of its pits of backwardness and deprivation, uncover the egotistic interests in public sectors and denounce them?

> The congestion and the thousands of citizens who wait long hours for public transport; the price increases and price gouging and speculation; the monopoly that produces the chronic housing crises in the cities of Syria that have no equal;

the neglect and exploitation in the health services and the thousands of "illegal" automobiles that disrupt public order and that induce corruption: Are we seriously trying to solve these problems and many others or are we offering only superficial solutions? . . .

Many of our sons who are technicians and specialists in various fields are forced to emigrate abroad and they are given no opportunity to place their abilities at the disposal of the homeland . . .

A widening gap has been created between the incomes derived from work and those from capital gains and especially from commercial capital . . .

The Two Nationalisms in Syria

By JOSEPH NEYER

What is now called the American University of Beirut was founded in 1866 as the Syrian Protestant College. The recollection of the earlier designation of this influential educational institution provides two important elements in the historical perspective requisite for an understanding of the unhappy events of 1975-1976 in Lebanon. In the first place, it reminds us that the establishment of Lebanon as a sovereign state distinct from Syria was the consequence of the policies of France as mandatory power between the two World Wars; it is a relatively recent political creation and not necessarily a foregone conclusion today in the minds of certain Syrian statesmen.[1] Thus, when the Christian President of Lebanon travels to Damascus to work out the details of the new internal political arrangements for Lebanon with the assistance of the Syrian President, who gives assurances of his continued support of Lebanese sovereignty, one cannot help but call to mind the visitation of the Emperor Henry IV to the Pope at Canossa.

In the second place, the earlier designation of the University of Beirut reminds us of the role played by American Protestant missionaries in giving what is regarded by many Arab scholars as the initial impetus to modern Arab nationalism. David Finnie tells us that "it is straining things a bit to insist that people (missionaries) of Eli Smith's generation (1801-1857) had a seminal

Dr. Neyer was Chairman of the Department of Philosophy at Rutgers University for twelve years. He is one of the co-editors of The Palestinians: People, History, Politics (Transaction Press, 1975) and has contributed many articles to leading publications on philosophy and on the Middle East.

1. George Antonius informs us that by the term Syria, he means "the whole of the country of that name, which is now split up into the mandated territories of (French) Syria and the Lebanon, and British Palestine and Transjordan." The Arab Awakening–The Story of the Arab National Movement (Hamish Hamilton, London, 1945), p. 15, n. 1, first published in 1938.

influence on the development of Arab nationalism . . ."[2] However, Arab historians such as Antonius, Atiyah, Hitti, and Tibawi do testify to that "seminal influence."

The aims of the American missionaries in nineteenth century Syria were not clearly defined. Unlike missionaries from other lands, they did not come as instruments of national policy. They were (mostly) innocent Americans with the high purpose of improving the quality of life in accordance with their best Christian and puritan lights. In the service of their ambiguously formulated aims, they endured painful discomforts, experienced exotic diseases, and shortened their natural lives.

Early in the century these representatives of American Protestantism perceived that the direct conversion of Muslims to Christianity could have no place in their endeavors. The Turkish administrators would not otherwise have tolerated their presence; and the penalty for apostasy from Islam was death and public mutilation. Rather, the missionaries directed their efforts toward the reformation of the Christians of the Eastern Churches—the Greek Orthodox, the Armenian Orthodox, the Nestorians, the Maronites, and (perhaps) the small foreign enclaves of Roman Catholicism; the hope was that *eventually* a reformed Christian community might be more endowed with the meritorious qualities requisite for reaching the Islamic community. Occasionally, the eastern Christian patriarchs appealed to the Ottoman (Islamic) authorities, in the interests of social order, to check the activities of the Americans, who in their turn appealed for ":protection" to the foreign powers with influence upon Constantinople—usually the British.[3]

The American missionaries arrived on the Syrian scene in numbers, especially during the temporary reign of Muhammad Ali and his son Ibrahim,[4] whose work of social reorganization had created, until their downfall in 1840, an encouraging atmosphere of tolerance. The year 1834 is often mentioned as a

---

2. David H. Finnie, *Pioneers East–The Early American Experience in the Middle East,* Harvard Middle Eastern Studies 13 (Harvard University Press, Cambridge, Mass., 1967), p. 135. In taking this view, Finnie is apparently leaning upon George E. Kirk, *A Short History of the Middle East* (London, 1948).

3. David H. Finnie, *Op. cit.,* pp. 123-125.

4. Muhammad Ali had been a young officer in the Albanian military force assigned by the Turkish Sultan in 1799 to oppose Napoleon's invasion of Egypt. Soon after defeating the Albanians, the French withdrew from Egypt, and Muhammad Ali became master of Egypt by 1805. His moves into the Arab lands and into other areas troublesome for the Sultan were often of such a nature as to leave no doubt as to whether he was acting for the Sultan or for himself. His son Ibrahim, who was more identified with Arabism than he, established an administration over Syria from 1832 to 1840—with Muhammad Ali recognized by the Sultan as Governor of Syria. For a time, Ibrahim was regarded by the Syrians as a liberator. Probably the main cause of his downfall was the need of British imperialism to strengthen the position of the Turkish Sultan. And the Muslim population of Syria was not ready for a modern national state which established equality for its citizens regardless of religious confession. Here lay the basic ambivalence of the Syrian Muslims, since they also aspired to the establishment of an *Arab* empire, emancipated from Turkish rule.

time of influx of competing Catholic and American Presbyterian missionaries. The Americans found a Syria whose political and social organization rested upon sectarian distinctions; the Christians occupied a distinctly inferior position—"subjected to invidious laws of exception which operated to their detriment in matters of taxation, justice and other rights of citizenship."[5] David Landes sums up an important aspect of the situation in which the Americans found themselves, when he says that "the history of Muslim-Christian relations in the Ottoman Empire in the course of the nineteenth century was one of sporadic explosions of wrath by the Muslim majority in response to Christian pretensions to equality and self-assertion."[6]

What the American missionaries contributed to this explosive equilibrium seems to have followed from their conviction that the Bible should be read and studied in the vernacular. When Eli Smith,[7] one of the most energetic and creative of the early American missionaries, arrived in Beirut in 1827, he went off into the mountains for a year to study Arabic, a most unusual step for a missionary (European or American), and then played an important role in the introduction of the practice of teaching in Arabic. In 1834, the American mission's printing press was moved from Malta to Beirut, and Smith and his colleagues proceeded to create a supply of textbooks and teaching manuals. No longer would a schoolboy be punished for slipping from English (or French) into Arabic during class instruction. The last nine years of Smith's life (1848-1857) were devoted to his translation of the Bible, which was completed by others in 1864. This Protestant Arabic Bible was adopted by Arab Christians of diverse sects (including even Egyptian Copts) and has been in use for a good part of a century.

It would be misleading to suggest that non-Protestant Christian institutions in Syria played no role in this revival of the Arabic language. The Jesuits and Lazarists were on the scene two centuries earlier than the American Presbyterians, and there were Maronite institutions of higher learning founded in the eighteenth century. Besides cultivating theological studies, these institutions encouraged the study of Arab literature, and, indeed, some of the Arab scholars who eventually collaborated in the work of the Americans—such as Nasif Yazeji and Butrus Bustani[8]—received their early training and spiritual nourishment in these centers of learning. It was the American endeavor, however, that took the lead in developing the literature required for teaching school subjects *in* Arabic.

5. George Antonius, *Op. cit.,* p. 32.

6. David Landes, "Palestine Before the Zionists," *Commentary,* Vol. 61, 2, February 1976, p. 53.

7. David Finnie, *Op. cit.,* pp. 196-202. George Antonius, *Op. cit.,* p. 36, n.1, pp. 41-42.

8. Bustani became a Presbyterian and played a very important role in Eli Smith's work of Bible translation. For this purpose, he learned Hebrew, Aramaic, Greek, and Syriac.

In so doing, the Americans, wittingly or not, were entering into the heart of the tension between the Arabs and their Turkish rulers, for the language issue was an important part of the Arab demand for "autonomy." As one Arab analyst of nationalist ideas puts the matter, "Arab Muslims were compelled to attend government schools where Turkish was the medium of instruction. This educational policy left the Arabic language with only one refuge, the Christian missionary establishments. Hence their great contribution to the Arab revival."[9] Or, as historian Atiyah celebrates the coming into being of Arab nationalism, after his discussion of the failure of Muhammad Ali and his son Ibrahim to have a lasting effect in Syria, "It was only later in the century that Arab national consciousness began to awaken throughout the Arab world, called to life not by the exploits of a military leader, but by the message of a rediscovered culture."[10]

It became the hope of the Christian Arabs that through the rediscovery of, and emphasis upon, the common Arabic heritage—and also the development of western ideas of nationalism—they would find the way to emancipation from Ottoman rule. At the same time, they would develop values that could be shared with their Muslim neighbors so as to render a pacific and productive coexistence feasible. The message preached by Yazeji at his home to large groups of followers was that they must revivify the common Arab inheritance, upon which a "fraternal" future could be built. In the air was a kind of "positivistic" faith in the rewards of literacy and history and "science," which was assumed to be compatible with both Christianity and Islam.[11]

In 1847, the Society of Arts and Sciences was established in Beirut on the initiative of Yazeji and Bustani, with the cooperation of members of the American mission. By 1849, the Society had fifty members, most of whom were Syrian Christians living in Beirut; there were no Muslim or Druze members. Papers were read, discussed, and published in a volume of transactions. Other societies with similar aims came into being. The Society of Arts and Sciences lasted only five years, and one may hazard the guess that its short life could be explained by the fact that the need was felt for an organization which could enlist the energies of Muslims.[12]

9. Hazem Zaki Nuseibeh, *The Ideas of Arab Nationalism* (Cornell University Press, Ithaca, New York, 1959), p. 50.

10. Edward Atiyah, *The Arabs–The Origins, Present Conditions, and Prospects of the Arab World* (Pelican Books, Penguin Books, Harmondsworth, Middlesex, 1955), p. 78.

11. Similarities may be found, if the analogy is not pushed too far, with the contemporaneous *haskalah* in Jewish East Europe. In both cases, the intellectual and literary movements seemed to be necessary preludes to the development of nationalism. Both movements flirted with the European Enlightenment while exhibiting an ambivalent and "romantic" mood with regard to the "superstitious" past.

12. George Antonius has researched the activities of these early learned societies. *Op. cit.,* pp. 51-54.

Thus, in 1857, the Syrian Scientific Society came into being. It was proposed by Syrian Muslims, with the condition that its members be limited to Arabs; the missionary influence would thus be checked, but all creeds and sects would come together in the service of the advancement of learning. Although the initiative was taken by Muslims, the Syrian Society was energized by the appeals of the two Arab Christians, Yazeji and Bustani. The massacres of 1860 caused a hiatus in the activities of the Society, and yet its work was soon resumed by its more than one hundred and fifty members so that by 1868 it received official recognition. The mood of these milieux is perhaps expressed by the fact that, in the wake of the massacres, Bustani founded a newspaper, *Clarion of Syria,* for the purpose of teaching the doctrine that knowledge and enlightenment can destroy bigotry and contribute to the realization of common ideals—shared by persons of different religious creeds.

At a closed meeting of eight members of the Syrian Scientific Society, Ibrahim Yazeji, son of Nasif Yazeji, recited his poem of liberation, which sang of past Arab achievements, condemned religious dissension, and looked forward to the rejection of Turkish rule. Unwritten, owing to its seditious character, it was memorized by those present and received a wide distribution— making its appeal to the ethnic pride of youth. It is understandable that Antonius should say, "The foundation of the Society was the first outward manifestation of a collective national consciousness, and its importance in history is that it was the cradle of a new political movement."[13]

What is called "Arab nationalism" today has a continuity with the "new political movement" that had its beginnings in the nineteenth century "scientific" societies. And yet the emotions of Arafat and Assad are quite definitely not those of Bustani and Yazeji. Very simply, what began as an effort of the Arab Christian minority to create a "nationalistic" *elan* that would enable them to join hands with the Muslims, developed into a movement having a recognizable Islamic character, so that both Muslims and Christians became less certain, as time went on, that the Christians were part of the movement. The sentiments of "patriotism" in the western sense, of devotion to a secular nation-state, which the Syrian Christians had attempted to cultivate, gradually found their place—became cognizable to the Muslims—in a complex of loyalties having a more ancient history than modern nationalism. Islam was not a "religion" among others that could be "separated" from the "state," in which the members of a plurality of religious congregations could coexist as "equal" citizens. For the Islamic community *is* the community *and* the "political" system *and* the relationship to the transcendental reality—all at once. This is related to the point made by Bernard Lewis when he says, "As the (Arab) nationalist movement has become genuinely popular, so it has become less national and more religious—in other words, less Arab and more Islamic. In

13. *Ibid,* p. 54.

moments of crisis . . . it is the instinctive communal loyalty which outweighs all others."[14] "The imported Western idea of ethnic and territorial nationhood remains, like secularism, alien and incompletely assimilated."[15]

It may be useful to make a few additional historical notes relevant to the withering away of the kind of nationalism cultivated by the early "scientific" societies.

The period following the withdrawal of the Egyptian rule[16] over Syria in 1840 was one of intermittent disturbances that may be regarded as the reaction of the population to the cessation of the legal equalitarianism among the sects that had been fostered by Ibrahim. The Muslims were reaffirming the "natural" superior status that belonged to Muslim subjects under a Caliph-Sultan, even if he be a Turkish Caliph. The Maronites (the majority of the Christians) looked to the French for support. The Druze looked to the British.[17] There was push and pull in this triangularity of power and passion, the changing outcomes of which depended upon the changing relations of the Sultan to the European Powers.

In 1856, under British and French pressure, the *Hatti Humayun* was promulgated by the Sultan. This decree affirmed the equality of all creeds with regard to taxation and civil rights. It may be that the *Hatti Humayun* was a necessary condition of the founding of the Syrian Scientific Society in the following year. Also in the following year, disturbances developed which culminated in the conflagration of 1860, in which eleven thousand lives were lost; the massacre of the Christians of Damascus is said to have been one of the "most savage" in history.[18] Certain analogies to the civil war in Lebanon of 1975-76 may be drawn; thus, in both periods, the hostilities took on the aspects of economic class conflict and also of sectarian warfare. In 1860, what started as a Christian peasant revolt against both Christian and Druze landowners became a conflict of Druze peasantry and landlords against Christians in general; the events of 1860 do not appear to lend themselves to a "marxist" interpretation of the sectarian conflict.

Foreign warships and a French expeditionary force arrived on the scene. The Ottoman representatives met with European representatives in Beirut, thus

14. Bernard Lewis, "The Return of Islam," *Commentary*, 61, 1, January 1976, p. 44.

15. *Ibid*, p. 41. Cf. Hazem Zaki Nuseibeh, *Op. cit.*, p. 61. "The Arab nation . . . has only recently launched itself on a career of nationhood. As an Islamic community, its roots are deeply embedded in the past. Its legacy covers every field of human thought and interest. Its institutions, its symbols, its rituals, and its traditions are the work of countless generations. As a nation in the modern secular sense, the Arabs have to begin from scratch. In fact, they have to decide who an Arab is."

16. See *Supra*, note 4.

17. In a total Syrian population of 1½ million, the percentages of Muslims, Christians, and Druze were, respectively, 65%, 31%, 4%, according to the tentative figures offered by George Antonius, *Op. cit.*, p. 55, n. 1.

18. George Antonius, *Op. cit.*, p. 58.

setting a precedent for European intervention in the Lebanon; their negotiations led to a document know as the *Règlement Organique* of 1864. It was followed by the reorganization of the administrative arrangements for the Ottoman governance of Syria—providing for a special status for the Lebanon, taking into account the fact of its large Christian population.

It is probably fair to say that the tragic upheaval of 1860 registered itself in the minds of the inhabitants as an ungetoverable trauma of the type that inevitably transfigures the future. Antonius emphasizes its positive consequences—leading, for instance, "to an intensification of effort in favour of breaking down the barriers of obscurantism."[19] It is, however, possible also to regard the events of 1860 and the *Règlement Organique* of 1864 as signalling the beginning of the development of an *acceptance* of sectarian separation—even if, it is to be hoped, pacific. If the Muslims continue their rebellion against the Turkish Empire, it is less an opposition to Islamic rule, more a stand in favor of greater "decentralization" and autonomy—and, at times, the demand for a Caliphate that will be Arabic in character; it is a demand that the fate of Muslim Arabs in Syria should not be shaped by the relations of a corrupt Ottoman Sultan with his European patrons.

This is not to deny a continuity in the influence of the spirit of the Scientific Societies of mid-century—but with gradual transformation. In 1875, five young Syrian Christians created a secret society with revolutionary aims. The membership increased to twenty-two persons of different creeds, supposedly representing the enlightened *elite* of Syria. By 1880, they emerged into the light of day by the method of denouncing the evils of Turkish misrule on placards that were posted during the night in the streets of Beirut, Damascus, Tripoli, or Sidon. Antonius spends some pages in the analysis of the contents of the third placard, which appeared on December 31, 1880.[20] He mentions, but does not appear to attribute appropriate significance to the description on this placard of the Sultan's tenure of the Caliphate as a usurpation of Arab rights to the Caliphate; the Turks are accused of violating the "laws of Islam"—hardly an accusation one expects from a movement whose aim is a democratic secular state. The first plank of the program announced on the placard makes a demand for "the grant of independence to Syria in union with the Lebanon." Is this demand an expression of the spirit of the early "scientific societies" which sought to break down barriers, as Antonius suggests? Or is it (perhaps at the same time) an expression of Muslim concern about the loss of real estate to the future independent Arab state? Or is it a condemnation of the Sultan's subordination to the European Powers, which underlay the partial autonomy granted to a predominantly Christian Lebanon?

19. *Ibid*, pp. 59-60.
20. *Ibid*, pp. 83-88.

It is ironic that whereas in mid-century the cultivation of the Arab language and literature was, as has been noted, the concern of the Christians and the missionaries, yet toward the turn of the century there was a reversal in the linguistic behavior of Christians and Muslims. It was the Muslims whose educational institutions fostered the use of Arabic. The Christians, on the other hand, received a more advanced education in the schools and colleges supported by French, American, British, Russian, and German missions, in which each nationality utilized its own language. Partly, this linguistic pluralism was maintained as a consequence of imperialist rivalries served by some of the western educational endeavors. Partly, it was the consequence of the difficulties for Arabic created by the introduction of the modern western natural sciences into the curriculum. By 1880, even the Syrian Protestant College resorted to English as the instrument of its educational program. The Muslims tended to keep aloof from the foreign schools, they were concerned about the dangers of Christian theological influences, and they were willing to attend the Turkish colleges; thus, they remained closer to the Arabic heritage.

Antonius attributes to this educational situation the transfer of the leadership of the Arab national movement from Christian to Muslim hands.[21] However, a contrary hypothesis suggests itself: namely, that by this time the Christians were beginning to give up on the old hopes for national unity with the Muslims. Their readiness to develop closer ties with the foreign cultures signified an acceptance of the Muslim view of the importance of religion and a decision to depend on the protection of Christian powers.

Indeed, toward the turn of the century, there began to appear a number of Arab intellectuals and ideologists who sought a synthesis of Arab nationalism and Islamic revivalism.[22] One of the most interesting of these was Abdul Rahman al-Kawakebi, owing not only to his broad humanism and his humane preoccupations, but also to his readiness to hold together in one intellectual enterprise the apparently incompatible impulses required by his time and place. Kawakebi brings together Islamic revivalism, Arab nationalism, westernization, and constitutionalist reformism. While advocating the unity of Islam, he argued for the unique role of the Arabs and the need for an Arab caliphate; at the same time, he took his stand upon modern western rationalism. His ideological endeavors played their part in the Muslim assumption of leadership of the nationalist movement.

It is worth recalling that in 1875 the Syrian secret revolutionary society was created by five young Syrian Christians, while in 1911 the historically important revolutionary and secret *al-Fatat* was founded by seven young Muslim Arabs. The membership of al-Fatat soon grew to over 200 members, almost all of whom were Muslims. When the movement in Syria eventually made contact

21. *Ibid*, pp. 92-95.
22. See Hazem Zaki Nuseibeh, *Op. cit.*, pp. 119-147.

with the larger "Arab uprising," it was by sending an emissary of al-Fatat in 1915 to Hussein, Sharif and Emir of Mecca, guardian of the Holy Places of Islam in the Hejaz.[23] One of the sons of this descendant of the Prophet entered Damascus on October 3, 1918 with his army of 1,200 Bedouins of the southern desert—along with British General Allenby coming up from Jerusalem—thus signalling the conclusion of four hundred years of Ottoman rule.

Where were the spiritual descendants of Yazeji and Bustani during these historically momentous events? Although some of them lost their lives under Turkish martial law during World War I (presumably in the service of Arab nationalism), yet when the moment of truth presented itself at the close of the war, the majority of the Christians of Lebanon preferred to have France as a Mandatory Power, rather than to be a minority of an independent Arab state with a Muslim majority.[24] Historian Atiyah, who is a Lebanese Christian, testifies that during this decisive period the Christians in Lebanon and Syria had not forgotten the massacre of 1860.[25]

Of course the impression must not be conveyed that the Lebanese Christians were all of one mind with regard to their future. Some of them advocated a Lebanese Arab nationalism in which they would struggle with the Syrian Muslims for independence, in return for which the separate identity of Lebanon, Christian and more westernized, would be recognized, eventually, as a separate state. On the other hand, there were those who wanted to remain permanently as a French protectorate; some of these rationalized their position with the view that the Lebanese were of Phoenician and not of Arab origin. Then, as if to demonstrate the medieval Principle of Plenitude, there was the Syrian Popular Party, composed of young Christians who were unwilling to give up the old hope for Christian-Muslim unity; they desired to support a *Syrian* nationalism, but they laid down the condition that it not become part of a larger Arab nationalism; they wanted no part of the "primitive" southerners who had in 1918 acted as if they had liberated Damascus.

When France organized the administration of her Mandate after World War I,[26] she not only emphasized the separate status of Lebanon but she enlarged its area by including certain predominantly Muslim districts. At that time, she was definitely the foe of the Arab national movement, not only because she considered that its patron was Great Britain, but also because she feared the effects of its example in North Africa. In enlarging the area of Lebanon, she decreased the magnitude of its Christian majority, thus preparing the way for the hostilities of 1975-76; for at least part of the problem in 1975 lay in the fact

23. Great grandfather of King Hussein of Jordan.

24. See Edward Atiyah, *Op. cit.*, pp. 119-124, for a description of this situation.

25. Edward Atiyah, *Ibid*, p. 121.

26. For the events leading from 1918 to the independence of Lebanon and Syria following World War II, see George Lenczowski, *The Middle East in World Affairs* (Cornell University Press, Ithaca, New York, 1956), pp. 206-311.

that the Christians were no longer the majority, while the government had been structured constitutionally on the assumption of a Christian majority. It will be recalled that on more than one occasion during the civil war, some of the Christian parties suggested the possibility of a political solution through partition; in other words, they would accept a smaller Lebanon in order to avoid living in a country with a formally recognized Muslim majority. It would be difficult to understand the Syrian expressions of horror at this suggestion, unless one assumed that the Syrians have in prospect a very cozy relationship with Lebanon; Syria's warm embrace is big enough for all of Lebanon. What the Syrians said in response to the suggestion of partition was that another Israel is not wanted in the area: that is, another autonomous community that resists Muslim envelopment.

As a matter of fact, there has been for some time more sympathy for Israel among the Lebanese Christians than is manifest from what gets expressed through the obvious channels of communication. Harry Tanner, in a 2New York Times dispatch from Beirut dated February 10, 1976, reports concerning Lebanese Christians who "see some common interests between themselves and Israel." He quotes a young Maronite who said, "We have no links with Israel, but if you ask whether we identify with the Israelis as an embattled well-organized minority in the Middle East, the answer is yes."[27]

A long distance has been travelled since the Society of Arts and Sciences was organized in Beirut by Yazeji and Bustani with the encouragement of the American puritan Eli Smith. Who now clings to the hope of Christian-Muslim Arab unity? Perhaps Dr. George Habash and Nayef Hawatmeh, who lead the two marxist and most socially radical of the guerrilla groups and who are the only guerrilla leaders of Christian background. Perhaps, like certain Jewish revolutionaries in pre-revolutionary Russia, they refuse to accept their non-acceptance by the larger society; and so they expect it will wither away—like the state—in the classless society.[28]

27. *New York Times*, February 13, 1976, p. 3.

28. See Bernard Lewis, *Op. cit.*, p. 44. "Among the various organizations making up the Palestine Liberation Organization, the Fatah is overwhelmingly though not exclusively Muslim. On the other hand, many of the extremist organizations tend to be Christian, for in the radical extremism which they profess Christians still hope to find the acceptance and the equality which eluded them in nationalism."

II

Government and Ideology

Ba'th Party and Ideology

President Assad is the head of the regional (Syrian) Ba'th party. This party has been the dominating force in Syria's political life since the 1950s.

It is commonly accepted that the Ba'th,[1] (The Arab Resurrection [Renaissance] Party) was founded in 1940 by Michel 'Aflaq and Salah al-Din al-Bitar, two Damascus-born school teachers who had met while studying in Paris. The origins of their party can however be traced to the National Action League movement in Syria of the 1930s. This movement's efforts were directed at organizing Syrian youth along Nazi and fascist models and did not make great headway, but some of its ideas and especially its policy of non-cooperation with the French mandatory power remained attractive. There was a new effort, to create a National Arab Party, with a definite creed. Its tenets maintained that: 1) The Arabs are one nation; 2) The Arabs have one leader who will manifest in his person the Arab nations' potentialities; 3) Arabism is the national consciousness and 4) The Arab is master of (his) fate. This party did not survive for long either. Its founding spirit was Zaki al-Arsuzi, an 'Alawite living in Alexandretta. When that city was taken over by Turkey in 1939, Arsuzi fled to Damascus, where he gathered together a small group of exiles like himself and founded a party called the Ba'th. Arsuzi preached atheism but also believed in the mystical and humanistic values of religion and especially in the fundamental virtues of Islam and the glories of the Arab past. He was also greatly influenced by the Nazi emphasis on race and racial purity.

Arsuzi's role and influence on the thinking of Michel 'Aflaq was great, although the two men never mention one another in their writings. Arsuzi nevertheless created the climate of thought that gave the newly formed 'Aflaq-Bitar Ba'th party the mystical and nationalist elements in its ideology (to which 'Aflaq, a Christian, added such themes as "suffering," "love" and "pain") and it was Arsuzi's defunct National Arab Party that gave 'Aflaq's new party its first sizeable group of members—all of them 'Alawites.

The al-Ba'th al 'arabi (Ba'th) soon came to attract the young educated members of the urban middle classes in Damascus and Beirut: the army officers, the students at universities and especially at high schools and the professional people and the intellectuals, and also gained recruits in Syria and Lebanon among the students from all the Arab states. It appeared to translate the aspirations for Arab unity of the Arab intelligentsia into practice; to provide a comprehensive program for action.

Unlike many other political parties in the Arab world, the Ba'th does not

1. Also known as the neo-Ba'th.

confine its program to any single Arab state. Its ideology is pan-Arab; it conceives of only one possible Arab Nation-State in the Arab world and regards the various Arab states as illegitimate and artificial creations of the colonial powers and as no more than regions of the unitary Arab state.

'Aflaq, the party's theoretician, stressed the validity of the concept of "The Arab Nation." He called the three objectives of the party: "Unity, Freedom and Socialism" and coined its central slogan: "One Arab Nation with an Eternal Mission." The Ba'th party, he advocated, was a revolutionary movement based on an ideology emanating from the spirit of Arab nationalism and concerned with overcoming the regression and degeneration into which the Arab world had been plunged. The party's main effort, he said, should be directed toward the rejuvenation of the Arab will—toward "Resurrection." Because, in the Ba'th ideology, the existing Arab states are not recognized as entities but only as regions of the Arab nation, the Ba'th created what it called "regional" branches (i.e. the individual Arab states). Each region is sub-divided into district branches (i.e. it deals with local state issues) and each branch is sub-divided into units. The units are made up of a number of cells which are responsible for day-to-day contacts with the people and which recruit new members.

Every region has an advisory body—a Congress—an executive, a regional command, and a secretary. The General Congress is made up of the national, all-Arab leadership and a Secretary-General. The regional Ba'th party deals with its local affairs while the General Congress deals with issues that affect the Arab nation as a whole. In Syria, Ba'thist opposition to the reigning dictator, Adib al-Shishakli, drove it underground in the early 1950s. When it merged with Haurani's Arab Socialist Party, the new Ba'th—the Arab Socialist Resurrection (Renaissance) Party—became the second largest organized party in the Syrian Assembly of October 1954. But a new phenomenon had now emerged: the Ba'thist army officer, two of whom had led the successful coup against Shishakli. The party's character underwent a change. It had the experience of clandestine activity and had become a party in which the military element predominated.

The party's influence began gaining ground in Jordan and Iraq. In Iraq, where it was underground, it joined with the communists against the government of Nuri al-Sa'id. In Syria, the Ba'thists became the chief proponents of the union with Egypt. When that was effected, in 1958, Ba'thist prestige grew immensely. The Ba'th now regarded itself as the future ideological base for President Nasser's popularity in the Arab world and believed that the Egyptian-Syrian union would inspire in Egypt the same ardor that had inspired them. For the Ba'th it seemed obvious that the union was the first stage in its declared long-term goal of comprehensive unity for all the Arabs.

Yet Nasser's first demand was that all parties, including the Ba'th, be dissolved and merged into a mass organization similar to the Egyptian National

Union. He was especially active in his repression of the Ba'th. In Syria—and Iraq—the party reverted to its former, underground activity.

In 1963, successive coups in Iraq and Syria installed Ba'th governments in these two states. Internal factionalism in the regional (Iraqi) leadership gave non-Ba'thist Iraqi officers the opportunity to oust the party from power within a very short time. The regional (Syrian) Ba'th survived, but this was mainly due to the ascendancy of the Ba'thist officers in the Syrian army.

Assad, who came to power in Syria via a coup,[2] is considered a "moderate" by the younger, more militant Ba'thist generation. He is also an 'Alawite, and the preponderance of 'Alawites in the army and the party bureaucracy and leadership points to the still sectarian character of the Syrian regime. 'Aflaq has long since repudiated his own party. He has accused its leaders of deviation from the pure principles of Ba'thism and of behaving like the Communists. Bitar, Haurani and 'Aflaq were accused of plotting against the Ba'th regime in 1969 and sentenced to death (in absentia).

The Ba'th party has had a turbulent career, filled with persistent internal divisions, conflicts, assassinations and coups. Because it advocates the existence of only one Arab nation (and has an underground network), it has tried to meddle in the internal affairs of all the Arab states while its radicalism has aroused their fear and suspicion. The party ideology declares that no Arab region can improve its condition in isolation from the other regions, but in practice this precept has led to inter-Arab clashes and divisiveness. Syria, where the Ba'th originated, has remained its main center—a fact that has led to a struggle between the "national" (all-Arab) and the "regional" commands. The rift became so deep in 1966 that the "national" headquarters of the party were transferred to Beirut and then to Baghdad—and because of the present hostility between Syria and Iraq, no Syrian representative of the Ba'th attends the "national" congresses in Baghdad.

Ideologically, one of its serious problems is the Ba'thist interpretation of "socialism," which had led to a conflict between its Marxist and non-Marxist members, for the Ba'th slogans still call for "Unity," "Freedom," and "Socialism" as well as "One Nation, the Bearer of an Eternal Mission," and for the struggle against capitalism and imperialism as well as against Zionism. Its propaganda to the non-Arab world stresses its "socialist" component (although without ever really defining what that is). Its internal propaganda stresses its pan-Arab nationalism. More serious still is the conflict stemming from its position on Islam. Although the Ba'thist ideology is formally secular, it is in fact deeply entangled in Islamic tradition. Islam is a social, political, legal and cultural system, and in Islamic theory, is the only legally acceptable code. 'Aflaq, born a Christian, acknowledged the debt of Arab nationalism to Islam but stressed only those aspects that are moral and spiritual in nature. His

2. Called, officially, "The Corrective Movement" of November 16, 1970.

Muslim ideological descendants are more torn in their attitudes. This conflict, between Islam and secularism manifested itself in Syria in 1973, in the form of widespread rioting against the proposed new Syrian Constitution. Although President Assad is a devout Muslim, and the Ba'th built more mosques in Syria within the three year period from 1967 to 1970 than were built in the previous thirty years,[3] all this still does not appear to have allayed the suspicions of the Muslim Brotherhood and other conservative elements which are still very strong in Syria. It has also not served to make Assad any the more acceptable to the more radical elements in his own party.

SOME BASIC BA'TH CONCEPTS

. . . the Arabs are called upon to use all their strength when dealing with the problems of the nation. They should not rest content to illuminate this problem by reason alone. Knowledge in itself is not capable of penetrating to the heart of the national problem . . . The processes of thought should be accompanied by the thrill of nerves, by the beating of the heart, the searching of the soul, the awakening of the senses, so that the discussion of the problem and its examination may lead to the right solution . . .

Salah al-Din al-Bitar, in a lecture in Kuwait. Muhadarat Salah al-Din al Baytar; Al-ihlaf fi'asr al-dharri (Kuwait, 1955).

The Communist philosophy is based on materialism and explains historical developments by the economic factor, which is for it all embracing. The philosophy of the Ba'th rejects this materialist philosophy and maintains that the ideal and spiritual factor is of decisive influence on the development of human society. The spiritual movements, therefore, such as Islam, which appeared on Arab soil are not alien to it and are not in contradiction to its philosophy.

Michel 'Aflaq, Fi sabil al-ba'th (Beirut, 1963).

. . . The relationship between them (Islam and Arab nationalism) is not like the one between another nation and another religion . . . Islam was created in the heart of Arabism . . .

Michel 'Aflaq

The Ba'th Arab Socialist party was the first movement in the Arab Homeland to give Arab unity its true revolutionary meaning, to combine the national and the socialist struggles and to represent the will of the Arab Nation and its aspiration to a future, linking it with its glorious past and qualifying it to play an appropriate part in the victory of the cause of the liberation of all peoples.

From: Preamble to the Syrian Constitution

3. See Bernard Lewis, "The Return of Islam," *Commentary*, Vol. 61, No. 1, Jan. 1976.

Political Parties

The National Progressive Front, headed by President Assad, was formed in March 1972 by a coalition of five parties:

> The Arab Socialist Renaissance (Ba'th) Party: (In power since 1963; supports militant Arab unity). Sec.-Gen. Pres. Hafez al-Assad;
> The Syrian Arab Socialist Union (Nasserite);
> The Socialist Union;
> The Arab Socialist Party: (A breakaway socialist party);
> The Communist Party of Syria: (Illegal: 300 members were arrested in December, 1975.)

Syria has been a fully independent country since April, 1946. The provisional constitution of 1969, as amended in February 1971, provides for separate executive, legislative and judicial branches. Most of the power is vested in the President of the Republic and the Regional (Syrian) Command of the pan-Arab Ba'th Party.

Religion and State in Syria

By A. R. KELIDAR

Syria is a country of many contrasts. Its society is one of the most heterogeneous in the Middle East and yet its leaders have been the most ardent proponents of a radical integrative political movement: Arab nationalism. It is a country created by accident rather than design, at least not by the design of its own people but by virtue of it becoming a French zone of influence in the settlement that followed the First World War. It became a State without foundations and has more or less remained so. But it has shown a remarkable ability to survive, even though it decided, of its own free will, to renounce its political sovereignty and territorial integrity for three years between 1958 and 1961 when it joined with Egypt to form the United Arab Republic.

When France took over the territory in 1920, and once the Arab Government of Emir Feisal had been ousted, there was an implicit recognition by the French of the fragmented nature of Syrian society. The country was divided into administrative units corresponding more or less to the religious and ethnic communities as well as to socio-economic considerations. A State of Greater Lebanon predominantly Christian was detached only to become independent (independent from Syria not France). In the rest of the country, a State of Damascus and a State of Aleppo were later incorporated to form the State of Syria, where the population was overwhelmingly Sunni Muslim. A State for the Alawis in the region of Lataqia was also created, and the French set up a State for the Druzes in the Jabal region. The Senjaq of Alexandretta was given autonomy on account of its Turkish population. In addition, a special administrative region, the Jazira region, where the population comprised mainly Kurds, Armenians and other Christians, was formed. This arrangement continued until the signing of the Franco-Syrian treaty of 1936 when France acceded to nationalist demands to unite the country and grant it self-government. Indeed, independence was obtained on that basis in 1946. Thus all the constituent components of Syria, with the exception of Alexandretta which was ceded to Turkey by France in 1938, were merged to make up the present Republic of Syria.

In April 1973 some unusual slogans were put forward during religious riots in the central towns of Homs and Hama. The riots were not unusual by recent

Lecture given to the Royal Central Asian Society on 24 October 1973. Dr. Kelidar was born in Iraq and educated in Britain. He has been a lecturer in Middle East Politics at the School of Oriental and African Studies since 1966. His published work includes several contributions to journals and books, including the *Encyclopaedia of Islam*.

Reprinted by permission of *Asian Affairs*, Vol. 61 (New Series Vol. V) Part 1, February 1974, Journal of the Royal Central Asian Society, London.

Syrian standards. The Syrian Government at the time blamed Saudi and Libyan instigation; these riots were thought to have been encouraged and financed by the Saudis and Colonel Qadhafi of Libya against the socialist regime of the Ba'th Party. Riots have taken place at regular intervals in the last few years in protest against the socialist measures of the ruling Ba'th, the type of politics it has implemented, its alliance with the Communist Party in Syria and the Soviet Union in world power politics, and 'Alawi domination of the Ba'th Party. The slogans were, to quote only two: "Islam is our Constitution" and "There is no leader but Muhammad." These riots were the culmination of a campaign by the Sunni Muslim majority of the country against the 'Alawi dominated Ba'thist regime. The crisis was precipitated by the introduction of a new Constitution in the country.

Syrian governments have always been coalitions: Sunnis from Damascus, Aleppo and the central towns of Homs and Hama; Christians and Alawis from Lataqia; Druzes from the Jabal. It was an attempt to give every social element some representation. The dominant community is Sunni Muslim, thus the President, that is until the assumption of power by General Hafez Assad in 1970, has always been a Sunni Muslim. One Christian was appointed Prime Minister in the early 1950s but no 'Alawi or non-Sunni Muslim had ever occupied the Presidency before. What has happened since 1966 is that the 'Alawis have found themselves in control of the Army and the Ba'th Party. 'Alawis and Druzes were always encouraged by France to join the Army. Prominent Sunnis became the officer class but because of the purges that took place in the late 1940s and early 1950s most of the Sunni officers transferred their talents to the political arena, especially after independence. It was a time when all Syrian officers had to wake up at the same time in the morning lest one of them would make a coup. Thus the Army came to be dominated by 'Alawi and Druze officers.

From 1966 to 1970 the strong man of the regime was General Salah J'did, an 'Alawi officer. J'did seems to have been aware of the opposition which might be engendered by his assumption of the Headship of State, and therefore he formed what amounted to a coalition of radicals representing the various communities. In fact he seems to have been content to occupy a nominal position, that of the Assistant Secretary-General of the Ba'th Party, while the President, Dr. Nuri ad-Din Atasi, and the Prime Minister, Dr. Zu'ayyin, were Sunnis. J'did apart, there were other 'Alawis in leading positions, such as Dr. Ibrahim Makhus, the Foreign Minister, and General Assad, who was then Defense Minister.

But things have changed since Assad took over in November 1970. When Assad emerged as the strong man of the regime, he was concerned, at least for a number of months, with the consolidation of his hold on political power in the country. He named a Sunni, Ahmad al-Khatib, as President. However, in March 1971 the General was nominated to be President for the following seven years by the Provisional Regional Command of the Ba'th Party. Until then Assad and his supporters had been engaged in restructuring not only the party apparatus but that of the State as well. He had been successful in concluding an alliance with the Communist Party as well as with a number of pan-Arab groupings including the pro-Egyptian Arab Socialist Union, led by another Atasi, Dr. Jamal al-Atasi.

In January 1973 the Syrian People's Assembly adopted a permanent Constitution to restore political normalcy and to pave the way for parliamentary elections in the following months. It was to be the culmination of General Assad's attempt to consolidate his political power and to provide his regime with the basis of legitimacy that would make it acceptable to the majority of Syrians. The Constitution is not unlike the provisional Constitution by which the country had been ruled since 1964, also introduced by a Ba'thist regime. The new document, however, unlike previous ones and the Constitutions of other Arab States, does not state that Islam is the State religion, but merely stipulates that Islamic jurisprudence shall be the main source of legislation. This deliberate oversight on the part of the regime caused the most serious riots, a crisis that shook the regime almost to its foundations. It provoked a clash between the Ba'thist regime and the predominantly Sunni population over the omission; religious leaders throughout the country protested and urged believers to boycott the plebiscite on the Constitution to take place in March 1973.

The issue was more than just a statement to the effect that Syria was a Muslim country. It also provided an occasion for the Sunni religious establishment to challenge the 'Alawi dominated Ba'thist regime. As mentioned above, Assad is the first non-Sunni President of Syria. His express profession in Arab nationalism—in its most radical form, that of the Ba'th Party—seems to have been to no avail. Also to no avail was the President's earlier attempt to allay Sunni Muslim fears in the appointment of a Sunni Vice-President, Mahmud al-Ayubi, [as] Prime Minister. Assad also appointed a Sunni Prime Minister, Abdel Rahman Khlaifawi, a man of Algerian descent whose family came to Syria in the nineteenth century with the exiled Amir Abdul Kader. A third Sunni, General Mustafa T'las, was given the important portfolio of Minister of Defense, with three carefully selected deputies: one is a Christian, one is an 'Alawi, and the third, his name would suggest, is either a Druze or a Kurd. The 'Alawi officer General Ali Zaza [became] Minister of the Interior. All these measures were obviously not sufficient, and the President was driven to make public expression of his belief in Islam. A book which shows that the 'Alawi sect is an integral part of Islam was published by the Government press and widely circulated by its agencies during the plebiscite campaign on the Constitution. In the following months the regime also published an edition of the Koran (the Muslim holy book popularly known as the "Assad Koran" because of the portrait of the President on its frontispiece). A compromise amendment to the effect that "Islam shall be the religion of the Head of State" failed to dampen rising religious fervor.

These conciliatory gestures did not placate the Muslim fundamentalists. Widespread rioting in Hama claimed a score of lives and resulted in the sacking of the offices of the Ba'th Party in the city. The regime became so concerned about these anti-Government demonstrations, which spread to Homs, Aleppo and Damascus, that the President had to entrust the charge of the military garrison in Hama to his brother. Soon after that the Syrian communications media began to play down the affair.

In April 1973 more religious riots broke out on the occasion of the Prophet's birthday. These troubles at Homs were soon to spread to other areas. The circumstances of the rioting at Homs in April were different from those at Hama in March, but the underlying causes were the same. The violence that plagued Syrian cities in the early months of [1973] was the expression of the displeasure and opposition of the country's Sunni majority towards the political dominance of members of the 'Alawi sect, who control not only the Army and Government departments but also party offices in the provincial towns. The Muslim fundamentalists came out to demand the insertion in the Constitution of a statement to the effect that the President should be a Sunni Muslim, and that Islam should be the religion of the Syrian State. Neither of these demands was accepted, and the Constitution stood as it was proposed by the regime.

The question is, why should a country that has adopted secular nationalism as its national ideology object to a President who belongs to a heterodox Muslim sect? The explanation lies in the position of the Sunni Muslim community in Islam. The Sunni Muslim majority of Damascus, Aleppo and the central towns of Homs and Hama flourished under the Ottoman Empire as merchants, religious teachers, provincial administrators and Ottoman Army officers who considered themselves the direct descendants and heirs of the first Umayyad Arab Kingdom in Damascus. The collapse of the Ottoman Empire was to offer the leaders the opportunity to assert the position of their community, a position of primacy in Islam. They came to the conclusion that they had a divine right, almost a God-given right, to lead the new community, now called a nation, especially in a political State. The writing of such men as al-Kawakibi and Rashid Rida, who called for the restoration of the caliphate to the Arabs because they were the better Muslims, must have encouraged the Sunni Muslim community to assert that right. I shall deal later with the writing of Bazzaz and 'Aflaq as a further indication of this assertion. The implication of this was that the Sunni community had a divine right to rule over Arabs. This right has now been enhanced by the fact that the new political élite was not only Muslim, and Sunni Muslim, but Arab too, just as the rule of the Prophet and the Umayyad were. They did not do this in the name of religion but of nationalism. However, in the nineteenth century and even up to today, nationalism has been more or less adapted as a mere device for the protection of the Muslim community which has given way to the Arab community today, whether it was the pan-Ottomanism of Sultan Abdel Aziz, the pan-Islamism of Abdel Hamid or the Arab nationalism of the Shariffian cause and its supporters. It was in the name of the political demands of Arab nationalism, namely independence and unity of all the Arabs, that the Sunni political leadership sought the independence of Syria. Paradoxically, they were not really interested in the independence or the sovereignty of the Syrian State. On the contrary, their primary aim was to disestablish the State (Republic) in favor of a larger Arab entity. Thus from their pre-eminent position they were to subvert the very State they came to lead by virtue of their belief in the desirability of an Arab union.

Apart from the Sunni Muslims, it was the Christian Arabs of Syria who became the real precursors of modern ideas. Those young men educated at the missionary schools readily accepted European notions of nationalism and national self-determination, but there was a special reason for them to do so. Their exclusion from the Ottoman body politic on account of their religion and because of the millet[1] system led them to advocate the establishment of a State based on the principles of secular nationalism. What was true of the Christians seems to have been also true of some sections of the 'Alawi and the Druze communities. These sectarian, rather secret, inward-looking communities have not, unlike the Christians, enjoyed the security of the millet system or the protection provided under the capitulations. On the contrary, they have been periodically persecuted by the Sunni political establishment, and they sought settlement in the mountainous regions for reasons of defensible security. This led in turn to a stronger communal cohesiveness.

They sought, along with the Sunni Muslims, the unity and independence of Syria, and an equal status and equal opportunities in the new State. But the Sunnis believed in their right to dominate the State and soon transformed the high hopes of the struggle for independence into a grievance. Thus the social conflict was to be reflected, perhaps magnified, in the political field, especially when the soldier-politician appeared on the scene.

Politics in Syria, at least at the national level, has always been a limited phenomenon, engaged in by only a few participants who are fragmented into factions and cliques. These groups constitute what used to be known as political parties and have become a cabal of army officers which, with their civilian supporters, make up the various factions of the Ba'th Party. For these groups, led by minority officers, the sectarian, communal and ethnic identification takes precedence over the wider political loyalty to Syria, the nation-state, especially when we bear in mind that even the Sunnis themselves are undermining the very State that they had come to dominate. Here we must look to Muslim political legacy for the reason. In Islam the concept of loyalty is not to a State but to the community *(umma)*, and because of this citizens of the new nation could not really develop the kind of loyalty which exists in Europe. This has

---

1. A religious community in the Ottoman Empire, usually used of the non Muslim communities, which had some measure of internal autonomy. (Eds.)

added to the complications of the Syrian Arab problem. This conflict over loyalty is the most important factor to the understanding of Syrian politics, especially the politics of minorities, because such primordial loyalties have repeatedly been exploited either by political parties or by the other Arab States who have connived from time to time to establish a prominent position in or even to take over the State of Syria, and who have succeeded in most cases in establishing a Syrian clientele for themselves.

There is little doubt that the most powerful and coherent social groups in Syria have been the landowners, the tribal and feudal chiefs and the merchant communities of Damascus and Aleppo which are predominantly Sunni. However, the rise since the end of the Second World War of a new social element, namely the intelligentsia—teachers, doctors, lawyers, army officers and students—came to challenge the power and authority of the traditional ruling groups and supplant their social and political influence. Radical movements such as the Ba'th Party and the *Parti Populaire Syriene* attracted considerable support, mainly because they advocated policies which seem more or less designed to undermine the basis of power of the traditional leadership of Syrian society.

These parties did not really deal with the basic discrepancy between Islam and nationalism, especially with the concept of the ideal State in Islam. The State in Islam (the government of the community) is an integral part of the divine law and therefore it is perfect and immutable. Because of this any given order is ordained by orthodoxy, would make criticism or opposition tantamount to subversion and constitute religious heresy. This lack of tolerance which seems to have been inherited by the nationalist school of thought has rendered difficult if not impossible the practical reconciliation and absorption of diverse social elements in society, particularly as the only community acknowledged of its rightful place in the Muslim divine law is the Orthodox Sunni.

In most cases Arab nationalists have used nationalist terminology, or the terminology of nationalism, to apply the basic Muslim concepts. It seems that their perception of the political realities of the new concept of the nation-state was to be overshadowed by their Islamic heritage and the traditional Muslim view of the State. The new idea of the nation as an organic political community irrespective of its constituent parts had to give way to the position of primacy of the Sunni Muslim community as ordained by orthodoxy. Thus when Sati' al-Husri, perhaps the most prominent ideologue of Arab nationalism, states that there is no freedom for the individual outside the nation and that man must be prepared to obliterate himself in his nation to achieve his liberation, it must be concluded that there is a certain adaptation of basic religious tenets. There is a striking resemblance between this and the call of the early Muslims to pagans and infidels to enter into the community of Islam for their own salvation. "Freedom" therefore in the nationalist campaign becomes the equivalent of "salvation" in the traditional religious drive. Such freedom or salvation could only be obtained within the believing community of Muslims as it was then, and that of the nationalists as it has become.

It was Bazzaz, an Iraqi (Husri was a Syrian), who attempted to accommodate Islam in Arab nationalist theoretical writing. It was his attempts that exposed the nature of Arab nationalism and provided an affirmation of the nationalist belief in the pre-eminent position of the Sunni community in Islam. Bazzaz asserted that nationalism and Islam went hand in hand in every respect. Nationalism was the assertion by the Arabs to resume the mission of Muhammad. Thus the Prophet becomes the founder of the Arab nation, and Islam is the product of the Arab national genius. But this kind of analysis leaves out the non-Muslim Arab, the non-Arab Muslim and the heterodox Muslim who is a Muslim as well as an Arab. Bazzaz had the solution for their dilemma too. They become Arabs when they recognize Muhammad as the hero of Arab nationalism and venerate Islam as the religion that enabled the Arab nation to assert its place in the world. However, to the non-Muslims Islam, even considered as the foundation of Arab nationalism, remains a religion which is practiced by a group of people which for centuries has regarded itself as the overlord of all the Arabs. To the non-Sunni Muslim, the heterodox sects, it is an implicit invitation to recognize Sunni Islam as the only right path. This may seem to be really a religious argument cloaked in secular terms, but Bazzaz persists. He states: "The non-Muslim Arab used to enjoy all his rights under the shadow of the Arab State. The loyal nationalists among the Arab Christians realize this, and know that Islam and the civilization which accompanied it are an indivisible part of our national heritage, and they must, as nationalists, cherish it as their brother Muslims cherish it." As Miss Sylvia Haim[2] remarked: "this is not the tone of an equal speaking to an equal, rather it is the voice of a tolerant superior aware of his station reassuring a timid subordinate."

M. 'Aflaq, the founder of the Ba'th Party, on the other hand is interested only in the political activism of the religion, in spite of all the romanticism he injects in his concept of nationalism. He wants nationalism to do for the Arabs what Islam had done for them in the name of religious salvation. If this analogy is to be taken seriously, then the Orthodox Muslim must conclude that if there is to be such a crusade, there is none who is better fitted and qualified to lead it than they themselves, not the Christian 'Aflaq, nor the 'Alawi Assad. President Qadhafi of Libya . . . seem[s] to show that [he is] so qualified.

2. Sylvia Haim, ed. *Arab Nationalism. An Anthology* (Berkeley, 1964), pp. 50-57.

III

Economy and Population

Geography and Economy

The Syrian Arab Republic borders on Turkey in the north, Iraq in the east and Israel,[1] Jordan, Lebanon and the Mediterranean in the south. The Mediterranean also forms its western border. In the north, the border between Syria and Turkey is marked by a single-track railway line running along the southern edge of the foothills, while its eastern and western borders are marked by straight lines drawn for convenience between salient points. These stretch to the headwaters of the Jordan River and follow the crest of the Anti-Lebanon hills toward the sea north of Tripoli. Syria has two main geographic zones. The narrow western zone consists of mountain ranges and valleys. The eastern zone consists of a broad and open platform dropping gradually and crossed diagonally by the Euphrates valley.

The Syrian Arab Republic is 71,000 square miles in area. Some one-third is desert or non-arable mountainous terrain; one-third is pasturable and one-third is arable land. Of the arable area, which consists of some 24,000 square miles, only some 10,000 square miles (14% of the total and 42% of the arable area) are under cultivation.

Over 80% of Syria's population lives in an area flanked by the Mediterranean Sea and Mount Hermon. The city of Aleppo, once the second town of the Ottoman Empire and still the second largest city in Syria, is in this area. The capital city, Damascus, which is irrigated by five streams and is famed for its clear fountains and gardens, is also situated in this area. The Jabal Druze, consisting mainly of a vast outpour of lava, is a sub-region of the area. It is fertile in the west, producing good cereal crops, but eastward the countryside is barren and isolated. Syria's whole eastern zone is mainly steppe or open desert, although the areas close to the banks of the Euphrates and Tigris rivers and their tributaries have benefited from local irrigation projects, which have permitted some cultivation.

The presence of hills rising parallel to the coast makes central and eastern Syria very hot in summer and moderately cold in winter. Snow lies on the hills from late December to April and even May. The Syrian steppe passes quickly into true desert and most of Syria has an annual rainfall of under ten inches. The narrow band of territory where the annual rainfall is between eight and fifteen inches is sometimes referred to as the "Fertile Crescent" (it runs in an arc along the inner side of the hills from Jordan through western and northern Syria and east to Iraq). The Fertile Crescent has, at various periods in the history of the Middle East, been converted by irrigation and efficient organization into rich and productive land—as was the case in the days of the Arab caliphate.

---

1. Called "Palestine" on Syrian maps.

Small-scale modern irrigation projects have converted former steppe into land capable of producing cotton, cereals and fruit and surplus agricultural products have been exported to Jordan and Lebanon. The Euphrates Dam project was planned to place large new areas under cultivation.

The Syrian economy is significantly dependent on agriculture, which accounts for some 30% of the total national income. The major crops are wheat, barley, cotton and olives. Sorghum, corn, sugar-beet and tobacco are also grown and sheep, goats and cattle are raised. The main industrial branches are textiles, hide processing, tobacco, edible oils and cement. The main industrial areas are in Damascus, Aleppo, Homs and Lataqia.

Some 50% of Syria's population is 14 years old and under. Rural manpower constitutes slightly over 62% of the country's total manpower while industry employs some 13%. The per capita G.N.P. for 1972 was $320; it grew at an average annual rate of 3.4% during the period 1960-1972.[2]

Oil was discovered in northeast Syria in the 1950s. It is produced by the government-owned Syrian General Petroleum Corporation and yields some ten million barrels per year.[3] Following the discovery of new oil resources, Syria's oil minister, Adnan Mustafa, announced on May 17, 1975, that Syria would be joining OPEC.

In 1968, a 400 mile, 5 million ton pipeline was completed from the oil fields in the east to the refinery at Homs and from there to the oil port of Tartous. Other pipelines cross Syrian territory: the Iraq Petroleum Company pipeline at Kirkuk branches out at Homs to Tripoli in Lebanon and Baniyas in Syria. The "tapline" from Aramco's fields in Saudi Arabia goes through Syrian territory to Sidon in Lebanon. The Syrian government receives transit royalties.

Syria's largest development project is the Euphrates Dam, constructed with Soviet aid. Its Third Five Year Plan (1971-1975) included major investment proposals for the development of hydroelectric and irrigation projects and for the expansion of the various petroleum development projects, but Syria lacks trained manpower and relies mainly on the Soviet Union to provide the experts and economic assistance needed for its development.[4]

> The Syrian government English-language publication. *Flash of Damascus*, (No. 48 of November 1975) reported that the Syrian Council of Ministers had completed a study of the General Budget on October 31, 1975 and that this amounted to 16.5 billion Syrian pounds,[5] of which 10.5 billion Syrian pounds had been earmarked for diverse development projects in the industrial, economic, agricultural and petroleum as well as other sectors.

2. *World Bank Atlas*, 1974.

3. According to the *U.N. Monthly Bulletin of Statistics*, Syria's crude oil production rose from a monthly average of 86,000 metric tons in 1968 to 781,000 metric tons in June, 1975.

4. Syria is reported to have received $26.5 million from the U.S. in 1975 in economic development assistance, according to Morris Amitay, Executive Director, American Israel Public Affairs Committee, in *Testimony Before the House International Relations Committee*, November 10, 1975.

5. The July 1975 rate of exchange was 3.70 Syrian pounds per $U.S.

As a result of the increase in revenue, *Flash* reported, the amount of foreign exchange and gold reserves reached the figure of $755 million at the end of 1974 as compared with $478 million in 1973. To meet the effects of inflation of the last few years, the government had increased salaries and wages by 20%-25%.

Flash also reported that the number of elementary school students in Syria was 110,088, the number of students in intermediate schools was 307,452 and the number of students in secondary schools was 108,346 in the 1973-74 academic year.

Population

The Syrian Arab Republic has a population of 6.5 million[1] and also one of the world's highest birth rates. Syria's official language is Arabic, which is spoken by most Syrians, but there are also concentrations of people speaking Kurdish, Armenian, Syriac, Turkish and Aramaic. 90% of the population is Muslim. Of this figure, some 70% is Sunni(te) Muslim.

The 'Alawite community is the largest ethno-religious minority group, living mainly in the northwest. Syria's Druze population lives mainly in the south. Some 10% of the population is Christian and is divided into various sects: the Greek Orthodox, the Armenian Orthodox, the Syrian Orthodox, the Greek Catholic, the Armenian Catholic, the Syrian Catholic, the Maronites, the Protestants, the Nestorians, the Latins, the Chaldeans. A large section of the Syrian Orthodox and the Syrian Catholic communities speaks Syriac as well as Arabic.

Other religious communities are: the Isma'ilis (whose spiritual head is the Aga Khan); the Shi'i(tes) (known as *Mutawalis* in Syria); the Yazidis; the Jews. In addition there are also nomadic Bedouin who constitute some 2-3% of the population.

Several thousand Assyrians fled to settle in Syria after a massacre of their community in Iraq in 1933. They are Christians and Syriac and Arabic-speaking.

The Kurdish community settled in Syria in the 1920s, is Sunni Muslim and Kurdish and Arabic-speaking.

Syria's small Turcoman community is also Arabic-speaking.

Syria's Circassian community was settled along the western edge of the Syrian desert by the Ottoman government.

Syria has a Palestinian refugee population of some 138,000. Some 350,000 Syrians are permanent residents in Lebanon and some 315,000 are temporary residents in that country.[2]

1. According to a Demographic Survey conducted by the Syrian Ministry for Social Affairs, 1975. The Survey also cited the illiteracy rate as 57%. The *U.N. Monthly Bulletin of Statistics,* December 1975, gives the population figure as 7.12 million in 1974 (as compared with 6.89 million in 1973). *Air Force Magazine* (December 1975) cites the population figure as 7,370,700.

2. According to a Survey of the Lebanese population published in *al-Anwar,* Beirut, December 8, 1975.

'Alawites

The 'Alawites (also, 'Alawis or Nusseiris)—Syria's largest ethnic minority group—live mainly on the Syrian coast, in Alexandretta and in Cilicia. There are also small communities in Lebanon.

The 500-600,000 Syrian 'Alawites comprise 75% of the total 'Alawite population and constitute 11.5% of Syria's total population. The majority lives in the mountain villages of the Lataqia district, which is also known as the 'Alawite region, or the Mountain of the Nusseiris. They are, however, a minority of the population in the district's capital, Lataqia.

The 'Alawites are believed to be the remnants of an ancient Canaanite people and were influenced by Christianity and Islam. They adopted Arabic as their language in the Middle Ages and also the Islamic faith (in the version of the *Isma'iliyya* sect)[1] but broke away to create their own sect. The 'Alawites have certain secret concepts which are known only to a closed circle of the initiated. They believe in a Holy Trinity of 'Ali, the Prophet Muhammad and Salman al-Farisi (one of the Prophet's Companions). Until the mid-nineteenth century, the community enjoyed a measure of autonomy under Ottoman rule. The French made their region an autonomous territory—or state—within the framework of the Mandate but ruled by a French governor. The 'Alawite state became part of Syria (with partial autonomy) in 1936 but that autonomy was lost when the French Mandate ended in 1944.

The Syrian army has a much larger percentage of 'Alawites (especially in its officers' corps) than of other ethnic communities. Most 'Alawite officers come from the villages (most Sunni-Muslim officers come from the towns). Many 'Alawites joined the Ba'th Party because of its emphasis on nationalist-secular values rather than Islamic ties and traditions and 'Alawites have therefore also come to constitute a disproportionately large number of Syria's political leaders as compared with the other communities.

The fact that the 'Alawites are not ethnically "true" Arabs but only converts to Islam has given them an inbred sense of lostness. These feelings surfaced during the union of Syria with Egypt—the leaders of the coup that overthrew the union were mainly 'Alawite officers.

President Assad, a devout Muslim as well as a Ba'thist, appears still to share this sense of estrangement from the (Sunni) "Arab" element and an awareness of his status as an 'Alawite, as would appear to be evident in the numerous purges he has carried out in the army and the government since his coming to power.

---

1. President Assad won recognition for the 'Alawites from the religious leaders of the Shi'ite sect in Lebanon, who certified that 'Alawites are Shi'ite Muslims.

The Status of the Kurds in Syria

By OMRAN YAHYA FEILI

The Kurds who are one of the oldest people on earth are the direct descendants of the ancient Medes. They have lived in Kurdistan at least since 2,000 B.C. Their mountainous home lies between Iran, Turkey, Soviet Transcaucasia and Syria. Their language belongs to the Iranian family of Indo-European languages while their religion is nominally Muslim (their religious beliefs having declined as their movement for Kurdish nationalism has increased).

A community of some 500,000 Kurds (10% of the Syrian population) lives in Syria.[1] They were cut off from their kinsmen, the Kermanji and Zaza Kurds, by the artificial border drawn up by France upon its creation of the state of Syria in 1936. Syria's struggle for independence from the Ottoman Empire was led chiefly by Abdal Rahman Kawakibi, a Syrian Kurd who opposed the despotism of Sultan Abdulhamid. Among other prominent Syrian Kurds is Khalid Bekdash, the founder and Secretary General of the Communist Party in Syria, the first party in the Arab world which repudiated the idea of the destruction of the state of Israel and the only party within Syria which recognizes the existence of the Kurds. However, the party has changed its policy periodically with the changes in the Moscow line.

None of the four states bordering on Kurdistan has treated its Kurdish population in any but a brutal and oppressive manner. Their treatment at the hands of Iraq has been the worst, but Syrian measures against its Kurdish minority which began in the early 1950s and reached its peak (where it still continues) during the Syrian-Egyptian union have been harsh and repressive. In 1957 Lieutenant Hillal, a member of the Central Committee of the Syrian Ba'th Party from Haleb, who was garrisoned in *Jebal el Kurd* ("Mountain of the Kurds") wrote a report to Nasser suggesting a comprehensive plan to disperse and exterminate the Kurdish people. He proposed isolating the Kurdish region by drawing an imaginary political line which he called the "Arab Belt" *(Al Hezam el Arabi)* for the purpose of the application of special laws. Chief among these was a program of "land reform" which declared all deeds to ownership of land, houses, stores, etc., "null and void." The plan was implemented and the government assumed ownership of all these properties "on behalf of the people". It was claimed that the intention of the new law was to take from the rich and give to the poor, i.e., that it was the realization of "Arab Socialism." In reality, the properties were taken from Kurdish owners and distributed among nomadic Arab tribes brought from the *Badiyet el Shaam* desert and settled in the Kurdish region.

Mr. Feili was a lecturer at Brooklyn College and is a Ph.D. candidate in Economics at New York University.

1. This figure is 30 years old. No census has been taken since then.

A second repressive measure which grew out of Hillal's policy was the abrogation of all citizenship certificates within the Kurdish region on the grounds that they had been issued by the imperialist-inspired governments of the past and that they should be replaced by new, authentic citizenship papers. With the enactment of this law and the concommitant fake census of 1962, 90% of the Kurds in Syria lost their citizenship. Nasser was so impressed with Hillal's ingenuity that he made him a minister of state in charge of *Jebal el Kurd* which was officially renamed *El Mohafaza el Shemalieh* ("The Northern Province").

Because Syria's education system is state-run and Syrian law rules that only citizens may attend state schools, Kurdish children were deprived of schooling with the enactment of Hillal's laws. The economic disaster resulting from these laws has also had serious social consequences for the Kurds. There has been a considerable number of divorces, suicides and a high rate of mental disorders. A number of Kurds moved to Damascus—where they were quarantined in the Salihiyeh ghetto. 50,000 Kurds fled to Lebanon where they were granted permanent resident status but not citizenship, while several thousand settled in Jordan. Despite all their disadvantages, the Kurds are nonetheless eligible for compulsory military service in the Syrian army. In the Arab-Israel war of October 1973, Kurds were placed in the front lines as a shield to protect the rest of the Syrian army. These Kurdish conscripts were used to launch the initial attacks, and those who refused were shot in the back as cowards, while those who obeyed were the first to be killed by the Israelis. Much the same situation prevails at present on Syria's border with Iraq. Several thousand Kurds from Kurdistan have been granted political asylum in Syria, but on condition that they be stationed on the border with Iraq. Some 4,000-7,000 Kurdish soldiers are at present stationed on that border. Their leader is Jalal Talabani, who has been given a Syrian passport. The Kurds know however that their fate is prescribed by Syria's relations with Iraq.

Syria's program against the Kurds is not unlike that of the Third Reich. As a Nazi officer declared in 1943: ". . . it is necessary for us Germans to be at least double the numbers of the people of the contiguous countries. We are therefore obliged to destroy at least a third of their inhabitants. The only means is organized underfeeding, which in this case is better than machine guns."[2]

The Syrian Kurds, despite the repressive measures already described and the permanent garrison of 30,000 Syrian Arab soldiers stationed along the Kurdish border with Turkey and Iraq, have never ceased in their struggle for liberation and sheer survival. They can boast of Dr. Nur el Din Zaza, the founder and first president of the Kurdish Student Society in Europe and many other nationalist organizations, who has spent most of his time in prison since his return to Syria

2. Karl Rudolf Gerd von Rundstedt, "Address to the Reich War Academy," Berlin, 1943, as quoted in *Free World,* April, 1945.

in 1955. Jegar Kheween, the most famous of all Kurdish nationalists, whose patriotic poems are recited all over the Kurdish lands, is a Kurd from Syria who has been in exile living in various parts of Europe since the 1950s.

The United Nations has never attempted to remind Syria of its obligations to fulfill the binding tenets of the International Charter of Human Rights. If an international investigation were to be conducted, the facts disclosed would shock the conscience of all humanity.

> In its *Annual Report 1973-74*, Amnesty International stated that it had taken up "the cases of eight Syrian Kurds who were arrested in August 1973 for addressing a memorandum to President Assad in protest against the deportation of 120,000 Kurds as part of the Arab Belt Plan." The Report added that none of them had been tried, visits had not been allowed, and there were fears that they were being maltreated in prison.

The Status of the Jews in Syria

This ancient and once flourishing Jewish community still numbered nearly 30,000 persons in 1943. Today it consists of some 4,500, of whom about 3,000 reside in the capital of Damascus, some 1,200 in Aleppo and about 300 in Qamishly, a small community near the Turkish border.

Jewish life in Syria always was precarious and subject to the whims of intolerant rulers and easily inflamed masses. Under Ottoman rule there was greater tolerance, but there were still occasional threats to the community, especially during the declining years of the Empire.

Despite periodic difficulties, the Syrian Jewish communities produced numerous Jewish scholars and enjoyed a rich Jewish cultural life. Jews also played a prominent role in the commercial life of the country and in the professions. They continued to do so during the period of the French Mandate.

Emigration of Syrian Jews began in the 1880s—first to Egypt, Lebanon and Palestine and then to Latin America, the United States and England. Under the

From: Testimony Before the Special Subcommittee on Investigations, Committee on International Relations, House of Representatives, Congress of the United States, June 25, 1975. "The Current Situation of Syrian Jewry" by Dr. George Gruen, Director, Middle East Affairs, The American Jewish Committee.

Since this testimony was presented there have been some signs of improvement in the life of Syrian Jewry in such matters as education, employment and travel within the country. Jews are still forbidden to emigrate. The authorities have begun to issue new identity cards without the distinctive red marking "Musawi" (follower of Moses) but it is not clear whether these are being issued to all Jews or only a select few. The climate of fear and insecurity still exists. It would appear that the continuing spotlight of public attention that has been focused upon the problem of Syrian Jewry by responsible persons with a humanitarian concern for their plight and by representatives of the media has helped to bring about the measure of improvement at present discernable. *(According to Dr. Gruen, March, 1976)*

French Mandate, the Jews in Syria enjoyed full civil rights and equal opportunities. However, Zionist activities were forbidden. Gradual emigration continued in the 1920s and 30s, due largely to the deterioration in the political climate—as Arab nationalism became more intense and strife mounted between different ethnic and religious groups. During the Second World War, when the Vichy government in France collaborated with the Nazis, many Syrian Jews fled secretly to Palestine.

The Syrian Arabs were always vigorous supporters of Palestinian Arab nationalism, and when Syria became independent after World War II, physical attacks against Jews in Syria became more frequent and proclamations calling for a boycott against Syrian Jews were widely circulated. Anti-Zionist demonstrations became increasingly violent, with the local Jewish population serving as a convenient scapegoat.

After the United Nations in November 1947 voted to partition Palestine into an Arab and a Jewish state, anti-Jewish attacks reached a climax in Aleppo, when crowds pillaged the Jewish quarter of the city and set fire to stores, houses, the majority of the synagogues. Following the pogrom in Aleppo, other acts of violence against Syrian Jews occurred, the worst being explosions of bombs in the Jewish quarter of Damascus in February 1948 and in the synagogue during services on a Friday night in August 1949. The Syrian authorities prohibited Jewish emigration to Palestine and were reported to have given orders to shoot those found crossing the border illegally. The Syrians also imposed difficulties on Jewish travel to other countries. Nevertheless, thousands of Jews fled to Palestine or Lebanon and from there travelled to other countries.

After the establishment of the State of Israel in 1948, the situation of the Syrian Jews continued to deteriorate. Jews were forbidden to sell their property (1948) and Jewish bank accounts were frozen (1953). The Syrian authorities placed Palestinian Arab refugees in Jewish-owned homes in the Jewish quarters of Damascus and Aleppo and the embittered Palestinians often have harassed their Syrian Jewish neighbors.

Since then all Jewish emigration has been barred except for a few short periods of relaxation in 1949, 1954, (when Jews were permitted to leave Syria, on condition that they renounce all claim to their property) and 1958, (when they could leave on condition that they transfer their property to the Government). In 1959 those accused of helping Jews to leave Syria were put on trial.

The ruling Ba'th regime, in 1964, increased the official harassment to which Jews were subjected. They intensified internal travel restrictions on the Jews, requiring special permission from the secret police every time a Jew wished to travel from one city to another. They also vigorously enforced the regulation that identity cards of Jews be prominently marked in red on both sides: "Musawi" (of the faith of Moses). One of the purposes of such a special notation is to deny Jews the right, which other Syrians enjoy, to travel to neighboring Lebanon.

But travel is not the only right denied the Syrian Jews. Other documents of Syrian Jews carry similar special notations—their bank accounts, their certificates of membership in the medical guild, and even their licenses to operate motorcycles and automobiles. The numerous regulations and discriminatory actions against Syrian citizens who are Jewish are enforced by a special branch of the *Muhabarat* (intelligence or secret police) of the Ministry of Interior. Even in those areas where by law all Syrian citizens are officially treated equally, the *Muhabarat* exercises an arbitrary veto power. Thus, for example, there have been cases in which highly qualified Jewish high school graduates were denied permission by the *Muhabarat* to attend the university.

Similarly, for many years it was exceedingly difficult for Jews to obtain driver's licenses, and once obtained, such licenses have in some cases been arbitrarily revoked. Jews have also generally been unable to obtain licenses to engage in import and export, although a few have managed to continue in business by working together with a Muslim partner. Jews have found it difficult to obtain employment in government ministries, even in areas unrelated to security or defense.

Special discriminatory rules also continue to restrict the rights of Jews to sell or inherit property. In order to sell his house or his car, a Jew requires the prior permission of the *Muhabarat*. This is usually denied unless he can demonstrate that the purpose of the sale is to acquire a more expensive house or car. With regard to inheritance the law also discriminates against Jews. It is apparently a general rule that Syrians living outside the country cannot inherit property in Syria. However, in the case of Muslim and Christian Syrians, any heirs remaining in Syria divide the property. When a Jewish head of household dies, however, the shares of relatives who have left the country are confiscated by a special Palestinian Affairs Committee. As a result, in some cases the heirs remaining in Syria become minority shareholders and must pay rent simply for the privilege of remaining in their own homes. These discriminatory restrictions were imposed on Syrian Jews *before* the Six Day War of 1967.

No Syrian Jew has been convicted of espionage in the entire period of Israel's creation from 1948 to the present. Syrian Jews have, however, been imprisoned and tortured, often without formal trial, for having attempted to emigrate illegally—or for allegedly having helped other Jews to escape. Some Jews have been imprisoned for two months simply for having lost or misplaced their identity card. Others have been subjected to brutal interrogation simply at the whim of the secret police.

Syria is the only Arab country that totally refuses to allow its Jews to emigrate. In this, the Syrian Government's policy is inconsistent with Arab practice and contradicts the official Arab position which allegedly draws a distinction between Israel and the Jewish people.

In response to the pressure of world opinion, early in 1975, there was a slight liberalization to allow some blind or critically ill persons to travel abroad for urgent medical attention. Permission to travel *within* Syria has also been more readily obtainable than in the past.

In the spring of 1974 there was an international outcry following the disappearance and subsequent discovery of the bodies of two young Syrian Jewish men who had attempted to flee; and the rape and murder in March 1974 of four young Jewish women, in the mountains near the Lebanese border, as they were apparently attempting to flee the country. At first, Syrian Minister of the Interior Ali Zaza declared that two Jews and two Muslims had been arrested and had "confessed" to the murder of the women. After it was revealed that the two accused Jewish men, Yusef Shaluh and Azur Zalta, were respected members of the Jewish community (Zalta's brother is married to the sister of one of the victims), and that their "confessions" had been obtained through torture and were repudiated in court, the Syrian authorities first dropped the murder charge against the Jews, accusing them instead of aiding in illegally smuggling persons out of the country, and then last summer released them on bail. The two Muslims, with a record of smuggling and other crimes, were placed under psychiatric observation. The trial was scheduled to be resumed in October 1975, but there have been no reports of any further sessions thus far. This has prompted some authorities to believe that the Syrian authorities have decided to drop the proceedings against the Jews without publicity.

Moreover, after three years of imprisonment, the Syrian authorities also finally released two young Jews, Nissim Katri and Joseph Swed, who had been picked up by the *Muhabarat* in the summer of 1971. They had languished in solitary confinement in secret police cells without formal trial for nearly two years before being transferred to the regular al-Maze prison in Damascus, from which they were released in June 1974. Nothing is known of the fate of Dr. Albert Elia, Secretary-General of the Lebanese Jewish community, who was kidnapped from a Beirut street by agents of the Syrian secret police in September 1971 and was reliably reported to have been held in a Damascus military prison. He is presumed to have died in prison.

In addition to giving permission for a few persons to travel to Lebanon or Europe for urgent medical attention not obtainable in Syria, in the past few months the Syrian authorities have for the first time also permitted a couple of Syrian Jews to visit their family in the United States. But in all these cases they have had to leave large security deposits with the Syrian authorities, which are forfeited if they fail to return promptly. In addition, the Syrians required some close family members to remain behind, fearing that if the entire family were let out they would not return.

The Syrian authorities have singled out a few Jews for special privileged treatment. They are trotted out for display whenever visiting foreign dignitaries or journalists inquire about Syrian Jews.

For example, the *New York Times* on January 5, 1975 reported a Syrian statement that "the most popular men's clothing store in Damascus is owned by a Jew." This is true, but the *Times* failed to note that the owner, Halil Jijati, is known in the Jewish community to be closely connected with the head of the Syrian secret police. Mr. Jijati is also a member of the Jewish Community Council, which in Syria is *not* picked by the Jewish community but is appointed by the secret police. Because of his special relations with the police, Jijati has been able to rent space for his store in a government building and has been permitted to travel to Europe on business.

In 1975 three Syrian Government agents accompanied Mike Wallace of CBS' "60 Minutes" while he was permitted to interview a well-to-do family. Wallace noted that Mr. Nusseri is one of Damascus' best known artisans in copper and brass. His son, Albert, is a pharmacist. But Mr. Wallace failed to note that two other children of Mr. Nusseri had fled, leaving all their wealth behind because they wished to live in freedom. Moreover, Mr. Nusseri himself and members of his family had some years back spent over a month in prison for "interrogation" before being released without charges. Under such circumstances it should be obvious that Mr. Nusseri would not dare say anything critical of the Syrian authorities.

Similarly, the offer by President Assad to allow Syrian Jews in the United States to come and visit their relatives in Syria does not appear to be a realistic solution. Only one couple has thus far taken up the offer. Others have failed to do so, not only because of lingering fears as to how they themselves would be treated (especially if they left Syria "illegally"), but also because of fears of the possible repercussions upon their relatives left in Syria after they had returned to the United States. Syrian Jews are under orders not to discuss their situation with foreigners without first informing the *Muhabarat* and obtaining their permission. Reportedly after a Mexican Jew visited the Syrian Jewish community, all those he talked to were lengthily interrogated by the *Muhabarat*.

The Druze

The Druze (Druzes, also Druses) are an Arabic-speaking national-religious minority numbering some 350,000 living in Syria, Lebanon and Israel. The Druze sect is an offshoot of the *Isma'iliyya* and developed in the eleventh century around the Fatimid Caliph al-Hakim bi-Amr Illah, regarded by his followers as an incarnation of the Divine Spirit. The Druze settled on the slopes of Mount Hermon and later in the southern parts of Mount Lebanon where their emirs exercised an autonomous feudal rule. They clashed with the Maronites of Lebanon, notably in 1840 and 1860, when a Druze massacre of Maronites led to anti-Christian outbreaks spreading to Damascus. A French expeditionary force and the intervention of the other great powers led to the creation of a semi-autonomous district for the Druze of Mount Lebanon. Many Druze emigrated

to the Houran mountains in southern Syria where Druze had lived since the
eighteenth century. This region became the main Druze center and is known as
Jabal al-Druze (The Druze Mountain).

In 1921 the Jabal Druze territory was granted autonomy under the French
Mandate. A 1925 uprising in Syria spread to the Druze in the Mount Hermon
area (it was known as the Druze Rebellion) and became a national Syrian revolt.
It was put down by the French in 1927.

The French made Jabal Druze part of the Syrian republic in 1936, although
with partial autonomy. The region lost its special status when the French left
Syria.

The Druze in Syria number some 180,000, or 3% of the total population.
They form 80% of the population in Jabal Druz. Some 150,000 Druze live in
Lebanon and some 33,000 Druze live in Israel. The Druze in Israel joined with
the Jews in 1948 against the Arab invasion, serve in the Israeli army and are
Israeli citizens.

Some 10,000 Druze live in four villages near the June, 1974 U.N.-patrolled
Israeli-Syrian disengagement lines on the Israeli-occupied Golan Heights,
administered by an Israel army appointed military governor who is the senior
authority in the area, responsible for both branches of administration—military
and civilian. Each branch is headed by an army officer: the military arm handles
problems of security; the civilian arm coordinates all civilian activities, including economic and social services. The officers in charge of civilian activities
are seconded from, and work with, the respective Israeli Ministries, but are
themselves directly under the command of the military governor. The Syrian
legal system is still in effect in civilian affairs.

Agriculture is the main economic activity. The Syrians had regarded this area
as a military zone and permitted only that development required by the army.
Since 1967, mechanized farming techniques have been introduced and also
running water and electricity for every home. There is compulsory education, a
free high school for boys and girls and free medical treatment.

Under Syrian rule, the Druze on the Golan Heights were subject to severe
religious restrictions. There were no religious courts to govern the day-to-day
needs of the devout and even the most perfunctory ceremonies—such as
weddings—were subject to the prior permission of the Syrian authorities.
Religious ceremonies were curbed and gatherings at the tomb of El Yafouri,
one of the holiest of Druze sites were totally banned. These restrictions have all
been abolished.

There has been Israeli settlement on the Golan. Many are *Nahal* (para-
military outposts).

Cut off from their kinfolk by the exigencies of war, and uncertain about their
future, many of the Druze under Israeli occupation have openly asserted their
pro-Syrian sympathies—and these may be genuine or, understandably, an
expression of caution and wariness to safeguard their Syrian relatives and their

own families—if the area is returned to Syrian control. There have been cases of espionage but the general attitude may best have been voiced by their leader, Sheik Kamal Kanj:

> "Of course we are Syrians who wish we could return to live in Syria . . . But this is our home and these are our lands. We have no choice but to remain here."
> "We have to be neutrals in the Israeli-Arab dispute if we are to survive . . . We are like birds sitting on a fence. A strong wind can come along and blow us either way. Until we know what way the wind is going to blow, we have to sit where we are."

New York Times, Dec. 2, 1975

THE TREATMENT OF SYRIAN DISSIDENTS

A five-day conference in Baghdad in October 1975, which included Michel 'Aflaq, the exiled founder of the Ba'th, former Syrian President Amin al-Hafiz, former Syrian Prime Minister, Salah al-Bitar, former Chief of Intelligence Salah J'did, former Chief of Staff General Afif al-Bizri and many other Syrian exiles called on Amnesty International and on the U.N. Human Rights Committee to investigate the plight of some 1,000 Syrian detainees in prison and in special detention camps. It was claimed that more than 70 of them had died under interrogation.

The conference protested the execution of some fifty Ba'thists and Nasserists on charges of opposing the Assad regime. Among those executed, it was claimed, were Mohammed al-Hafiz, a cousin of the former President Amin al-Hafiz, Ali Saud al-Daoudi, Secretary of the Homs Ba'th Party, Sa'id al-Husain, a lecturer at Aleppo Technical College, Hazom al-Mufti, Secretary of the Hamma Ba'th Party, Salim al-Hamawi, lecturer at Damascus Law College and Mahmoud al-Rifai of Damascus University.

A former senior Syrian Cabinet minister went to London on October 15 carrying documentation and affidavits from some of those held in Syrian detention. The material has been given to various organizations together with an appeal for urgent action on their behalf by Amnesty and the U.N.

IV

Syrian-Arab Relations

The Euphrates Dam and
Syrian-Iraqi Relations

With the Tigris, the Karun and their common outlet into the Persian Gulf, the Shatt al-'Arab, the Euphrates forms the most important river system between the Nile and the Indus. It created Mesopotamia much like the Nile created Egypt. The source of the Euphrates is in Turkey and it flows through Iraq and Syria.

Iraq has completed two major development projects on the Euphrates designed for irrigation, flood control and power production. There is a similar project in Turkey. The completion of the first stage of the Soviet-aided Euphrates Dam project in Syria on July 5, 1973 followed fifteen years of largely abortive Syrian efforts to recruit financial and technical aid for its construction.

No agreement was reached however, between Turkey, Iraq and Syria regarding the allocation and use of the Euphrates waters. Iraq wanted 66% of the Euphrates water but the Syrians were only ready to agree to an Iraqi share of 55%, while the Turks, by building the Keban Dam across the river's upper reaches, placed themselves in a position to hold back as much water as they please. For Turkey, in addition, the Syrian Euphrates Dam project means that there is a significant Soviet presence in the vicinity of the Turkish border.

It is not the Turks, however, but the Iraqis who have embarked on a quarrel with the Syrians over the Euphrates' waters. In April 1975, Iraq complained that Syria was blocking the waters, thus endangering the lives of people and livestock. The Iraqis launched a propaganda war against the Assad regime and referred their complaint to the Arab League.

The growing tension led Saudi Arabia to initiate mediation efforts, but Syria withdrew from a committee that had been set up by the Arab League to resolve the conflict.

Reciprocal acts of aggressive confrontation were then committed, including the closing down of national air companies in both countries.

In June 1975, the Syrian government officially accused Iraq of concentrating large military forces including armor and missiles near their border. The Syrians closed the Iraqi consulate in Aleppo and accused the Iraqis of attempting to assassinate a Syrian Ba'th official and redeployed tanks, cannon and other heavy equipment guarded overhead by MIG jets from their destination on the Golan Heights (where they had agreed to an extension of the UNDOF mandate) to the Iraqi border. At the same time the Syrians claimed that they were only withholding one-third of the water and allowing two-thirds to flow into Iraq.

In July, the Syrian government ordered the closing of the office of the Iraqi military attaché in Damascus and notified the mission personnel that they must leave Syria within 48 hours. An Iraqi complaint to the Arab League said that Syrian warplanes had been overflying Iraqi airspace and that Syrian agents were obstructing the construction of a new Iraqi border checkpoint.

Syria retaliated by publishing the fact that mass executions were going on in Iraq.

Also in July, the Syrian Minister of the Interior, 'Ali Zaza, announced the arrest of most of the members of a clandestine group called "The Arab Communist Organization," hinting that the arrests might not put an end to the organization's activities because they had supporters "in other parts of the Arab world"—an allusion to Iraq.

Iraq complained of violations of its air space and reported that detachments of the Syrian camel corps and Syrian intelligence details had crossed into Iraqi territories and ambushed vehicles of the Iraqi border forces. It simultaneously revived its propaganda campaign against Syria, accusing it of "betrayal of the Palestinian cause" and of submitting "to imperialist plans."[1]

The Syrian Euphrates Dam project is planned to create a lake 50 miles long and storing, in its final stage, 40,000 mcm. This dam will irrigate over one million acres and create a power-generating capacity of over 600,000 kw., at an estimated cost of $600 million.[2]

---

1. Saudi Arabia, in the persons of oil minister Zaki Yamani and Crown Prince Fahd have tried to act as mediators in the dispute. In August, 1975, it was announced during Fahd's visit to Syria, that Syria had accepted a Saudi proposal for sharing the Euphrates waters with Iraq and that an agreement would be signed. Iraq had organized a conference of Palestinian groups in June, 1975. These groups—part of the "Rejectionist Front" (against Israel)—included: the *Popular Front for the Liberation of Palestine*, the *Arab Liberation Front*, the *Popular Struggle Front* and the *PFLP-National Command*. The leaders met in Baghdad with Iraqi Ba'thist officials.

On the night of January 31, 1976, Syria's Sa'iqa forces in Beirut attacked the office of two pro-Iraqi newspapers, killing seven, wounding seven and kidnapping five. The raid was carried out by a unit of some 100 men.

2. In June, 1975 the U.S. agreed to provide Syria with a loan of $58 million for water irrigation projects.

The Factors Behind the Syrian-Iraqi Dispute

By STEPHEN OREN

Since October 1975, the Syrian-Iraqi frontier has been quiet. No longer is the Syrian Army poised on the Iraqi front, no longer does Iraq complain that Syrian refusal to allow the Euphrates to flow downstream into Iraq endangers the crops of 3.5 million Iraqi peasants. Even the rhetorical interchange between Damascus and Baghdad has been toned down. In large part, Saudi pressure on Syria (which needs Saudi subsidies) to make concessions to Iraq is responsible. But the underlying suspicion and tension between Syria and Iraq continues.

The Syrian decision in 1974 to limit the amount of water that passes its new Tabaqa Dam on the Euphrates was the ostensible cause of the dispute. Both Syria and Iraq wish to use Euphrates water for irrigation and agricultural development. In both, such development would have the important political benefits of allowing ethnically non-Arab groups (e.g. Syria's Jezireh region) to be Arabized or of moving around potentially dissident minorities. There is not, however, enough water for both the Syrian and Iraqi plans—to say nothing of those of Turkey which shares the river with them. By limiting the flow, Syria hoped to put pressure on Baghdad to agree to Damascus' terms for division of Euphrates water if it wished to obtain any water at all.

Conflict over the Euphrates quickly became generalized. Iraq accused Syria of being prepared to betray the Palestinians by dealing with Israel. Syria retorted by asking what dark motive animated Iraq's "tribalists" to weaken a state on the front-line with Israel. Iraqi charges of unauthorized Syrian military . overflights and Syrian charges that Iraqi assassins had shot a member of the Syrian government certainly added to the tension. More seriously, the Syrians began to subsidize Jalal Talabani, a leftwing Kurdish leader, in his effort to renew the Kurdish insurrection in northern Iraq that had been destroyed by the Spring 1975 Iraq-Iran agreement. Needless to say, Syria continued its pressure on its own Kurds. In turn, the Iraqis have begun constructing an oil pipeline from the Iraqi oil fields through Turkey to the Turkish Mediterranean port of Iskanderoun. This added insult to injury, for not only does this pipeline bypass Syria (thus limiting Syrian revenues) but the Syrians continue to claim Iskanderoun.

The real source of tension between Syria and Iraq is not the oil pipeline, the Kurdish insurrection, military overflights, or even Euphrates water. Both Syria and Iraq are military dictatorships in which the ruling cliques operate in the name of the Ba'th with the other parties reduced to a distinctly subordinate

Dr. Oren is a specialist in Middle Eastern Affairs and the interplay of religion and politics.

position or simple illegality. But while the Ba'th claims to be a single unified party covering and uniting the entire Arab world, it is in fact split. Iraqi leader Saddam Hussein al-Tikriti and Syrian President Hafez al-Assad represent rival Ba'th factions.

Nevertheless, this is not an ideological feud. Despite all the discussions of "Arab socialism versus the Arab road to socialism" or the adoption of Marxist "scientific socialism," there is little real ideological difference between the two states. Both dictatorships have recently made some efforts toward liberalizing their economies and improving relations with their "non-revolutionary" neighbors. The pacts between Iraq and Iran in the Spring of 1975 and the Summer of 1975 reconciliation between Syria and Jordan are examples.

But both regimes wish to show themselves as the sole embodiment of revolutionary virtue and fear attempts to overthrow them. Both are minority regimes. It is not merely that neither would win an election—none will be held. While most Syrians are Sunni Muslims, the Ba'thist rulers are mainly members of the strong 'Alawite Muslim minority—a rather exotic Muslim sect which other Muslims profoundly distrust. In Iraq, the rulers are Sunni Muslim but most Arab Iraqis belong to the competing Shi'ite sect. While neither the Syrian nor the Iraqi leaders are noted for their specific religious devotion, they cannot escape the stigma of their religious identification. Nor is it surprising that it was the Syrian regime which took most of the steps toward confrontation. It is less secure, if only because 'Alawite dominance in Syria is only a thing of yesterday, of a decade, while Sunnis have run Iraq since the days of the Ottoman Empire.

Predicting the future of any Middle Eastern feud always presents a hazard. The sharp contrast between the shouted modern ideological slogans and the scarcely mentioned feuds and dislikes still determines much of Middle East politics. The inter-connectedness of internal and intra-Arab policies is a link that drastically reduces the Arab political leaders' freedom of action and this internecine bitterness that rules intra-Arab relations also points up the difficulty of achieving an Arab-Israeli accommodation.

Syria and Jordan

Syrian-Jordanian relations have had a checkered history. When King Abdallah, the grandfather of King Hussein, announced his Greater Syria scheme to link Syria, Lebanon and TransJordan in the late 1940s, this idea was in direct conflict with the old Syrian idea of creating a Fertile Crescent, which would include Jordan, Syria and Iraq. To Syria, Jordan was an integral part of Syria. Relations between the newly independent Syrian republic and the Hashemite kingdom were cool and often strained for some thirty years.

In the early 1960s the Jordanians claimed that Soviet-made MIG fighters of the Syrian air force had tried to force down an aircraft which was carrying Hussein through Syrian air space on a trip to Europe. When the Jordanian army fought the Palestinian commandoes in Jordan in September 1970, Syria led the whole Arab world in expressing its indignation. A year later Syrian armed forces aided the Palestinian forces in northern Jordan by reinforcing them with troops of the Palestine Liberation Army stationed in Syria. The PLO, supported by Syrian tanks, occupied northern areas in Jordan and the Syrian army only withdrew after the intervention of President Nasser, who convinced Syria that U.S. forces would intervene if it did not withdraw.

President Assad, upon coming to power, fostered improved relations with Jordan. During the Arab-Israel war of October 1973, Hussein sent the Jordanian Fortieth Armored Brigade to reinforce Syrian forces on the Golan Heights. It was, ironically, the same brigade which the Syrians had fought against two years earlier in northern Jordan.

A further improvement in relations followed the seventh Arab summit conference in Rabat in October 1974, where Hussein recognized the PLO as the sole representative of the Palestinians, including those living on the West Bank.[1]

The rapprochement between Syria and Jordan may well be one of the most interesting developments since October 1973. It reminded Egypt of the threat that Syrian-Jordanian military coordination could pose against Israel (although the existence of a joint Military Command [created in 1975] is played down)[2] and Assad's unprecedented visit to Amman in June 1975 stressed the diploma-

1. King Hussein, however, reconvened the Jordanian parliament, which also includes members from the West Bank, on February 5, 1976. The King had dissolved parliament in late 1974, following the Rabat decision. The constitutional amendment adopted empowered the King to convene further special sessions of the House of Representatives, the elected lower Chamber (half of them from the West Bank) and to act on additional amendments. (*New York Times,* February 6, 1976.)

2. The Syrian and Jordanian armies were reported to have conducted a major training exercise in Syria during the last week of December 1975. The exercise involved moving two Jordanian armored brigades—10,000 men—into Syria and placing them under Syrian command. The planning was done by a combined command.

tic rather than the practical significance of the new rapprochement—more attention was given, in their joint communique, to economic than to military affairs. The economic steps planned, if implemented, could be important to the development of both countries. A railway is to link the Syrian port of Lataqia with the oil-bearing region of al-Hasa in Saudi Arabia. A new highway will join Damascus and Amman. Air communications are to be stabilized and expanded. Jointly owned transportation companies will exploit these new potentialities. A free trade zone where the present railroad and the projected highway cross the border, is expected to act as a powerful stimulant to commerce. Syrian-Jordanian cooperation also includes plans for expanding existing undertakings. The project to harness the Yarmuk River, on the border between the two countries for example, is to be reshaped and enlarged. Citizens of either country will be permitted to cross the border without passports. It may well be that these new projects are meant as a threat to Egypt that an overland route can eliminate or bypass the Suez Canal.

Syrian-Jordanian relations have waxed and waned in past years. It still remains to be seen whether Syria can overcome the basically irreconcilable Jordanian-Palestinian positions and also how permanent an alliance between the two generally hostile countries can be.

Syria and Lebanon: The Background

By ELIZABETH L. CONROY

Relations between Syria and Lebanon, since independence in 1946, have been characterized by continuing tension over (1) economic matters, (2) asylum granted to political refugees, (3) differing positions on relations with the United States and the West, and (4) the conflict with Israel, including the role of the Palestinians in this conflict.

Very soon after achieving independence from France differences in economic policies led to difficulties between Syria and Lebanon. Two basic problems were involved: Lebanese and Syrian economies are basically competitive and not complementary, and the two countries have radically different approaches to economic policies. Syria has adopted "economic nationalism," or socialism, as the basis for its economy and Lebanon's policy is based on *laissez faire,* or free trade. During the Mandate period the two countries had a unified policy, including a common currency and customs administration. The

Ms. Conroy is a Ph.D. candidate at George Washington University's School of Public and International Affairs Graduate Program and a co-author of *The Persian Gulf* (Research Analysis Corporation, 1971) and *Area Handbook for Lebanon* (Foreign Area Studies, The American University, Washington, D.C. USGPO, 1974).

matter of customs fees produced friction since they were split proportionately, by size, with 44% going to Lebanon and 56% to Syria, while Lebanon produced the greater amount of trade revenue. The customs union (established in 1920) was dissolved in 1950, which precipitated tension requiring Arab League mediation. Lebanon's prosperity continued to grow with the development of a large tourist industry, with the attraction of foreign capital to Lebanese banks, and with the development of a transit trade of foreign goods from Lebanese ports to Syria, Iraq, Jordan and the Persian Gulf. On the other hand, political instability in Syria prohibited a similar development of the Syrian economy. Nevertheless, after two years of negotiations, an economic agreement was signed between the two countries in 1952. The agreement has, on occasion, been used as a weapon against Lebanon by Syria, which does this by raising the duties on goods being shipped from Lebanon through Syria. The Syrians have also used border closings as a means of exerting economic pressure on Lebanon.

Disagreements have been frequent over asylum granted by Lebanon to Syrian political refugees. In 1952 when Akram Haurani, Salah al-Din Bitar, and Michel 'Aflaq fled to Lebanon and mounted an attack on the Shishakli regime, Syria closed the border for 24 hours in protest. In 1956, during the Suez crisis, the discovery of a Lebanon-based plot against the Syrian government by Syrian Intelligence led to a deterioration in relations between the two countries. However, following Syria's secession from the United Arab Republic (UAR) in 1961, the Foreign Ministers of Syria and Lebanon reached an agreement on mutual cooperation in solving the problem of political subversion after discussions on the infiltration of UAR agents into Syria from Lebanon. Nevertheless, in 1968 Syria found it necessary to impose higher duties as well as a tax on trucks engaged in the transit trade, as a retaliatory measure designed to force the Lebanese to suppress subversion and sabotage against Syria that originated in Lebanon. These taxes remained in effect until the dispute was settled by arbitration by the Arab League and the Lebanese government warned Syrian nationals not to engage in public statements or political activities of any kind.

On the other hand, Syria has also served as a base for attempted political disruption in Lebanon. The most notable case was the Syrian intervention in the Lebanese civil war of 1958. At that time Lebanon was forced to complain to both the Arab League and the United Nations Security Council about Syrian actions. Syria was, at that time, a partner in the United Arab Republic and its policies were ostensibly formulated in Cairo. During the middle of May 1958, rioting broke out in protest against the possible revision of the Lebanese Constitution that would permit Lebanese President Chamoun to take office for a second six-year term, thus extending the tenure of a pro-Western government in Lebanon. Radio Cairo and Radio Damascus urged the Lebanese to sustain the revolt and urged President Chamoun to resign. Actual aid to anti-government forces in Lebanon came from the Syrian sector of the UAR. Lebanon accused

Syria of smuggling arms into Lebanon and also complained that armed groups of Syrians attacked customs posts on the border, that material support was given to rebel leaders, such as Kemal Jumblatt and his Druze followers, and that insurrectionists were being trained in camps on Syrian soil. On the 6th of June, Lebanese Foreign Minister Charles Malik formally complained to the United Nations that there had been substantial illegal intervention by the UAR in Lebanon; he cited specific instances of the amount and kind of aid given the insurgents. Nasser and the UAR denied the allegations and a United Nations observer force was dispatched to the border. The whole problem of Syrian intervention was, however, muted following the Iraqi *coup d'etat* on July 14th and the subsequent dispatch of United States troops to Lebanon by President Eisenhower at Lebanon's request.

The ties between Lebanon and the United States, and the West in general have also formed the focal point of dissension between Syria and Lebanon. Generally speaking, Lebanon's position was a reflection of its commercial interests and the need to preserve them by ties to the West. Its large Christian population also exerted its influence. This pro-Western stance has been anathema to the anti-imperialist, Muslim and strongly nationalistic Syrian leadership. The fact that Lebanon accepted the Eisenhower Doctrine in 1957 and that it asked for aid from the United States in 1958 made it vulnerable to Syrian accusations that Lebanon was consorting with the enemy. Furthermore, Lebanon's refusal to act as a "confrontation" state during the 1950s and 1960s had an impact on the relationship during that period. Furthermore, Lebanese repression of Palestinian guerrillas using southern Lebanon as a staging ground for attacks on Israel led to Syrian support for the Palestinians in their struggle against the Lebanese government as well as to infiltration of Sa'iqa (Syrian-based Palestinian commandos) into Lebanon early in 1969. The Lebanese army accused Sa'iqa of creating disturbances and prevented the Syrian commandos from crossing the border. The tension over Lebanese actions against the Palestinians grew; in October 1969 two large groups of armed Syrians attacked Lebanese border posts and the Syrian government again closed the border as a reaction against the attacks of the Lebanese army on Palestinian guerrillas in Lebanon. However, after the Cairo settlement of the Lebanese-Palestinian dispute in November 1969, Syria gradually reopened the border and *Radio Damascus* dropped its criticism.

During 1970 there was a considerable lessening of tension. Exchanges of visits by high level officials began at the initial invitation of the Syrian government. A Border Commission, which had been established in 1967, was reactivated and another Joint Commission was set up to resolve political and economic issues. By the end of that year all transit restrictions had been removed on goods from Lebanon going through Syria and Syria also abolished the requirement that Syrians obtain permits to travel in Lebanon. On the other hand, Lebanon restricted the activities of Syrian refugees against the Assad regime.

Relations between Lebanon and Syria continued to be good until May 1973 when fighting erupted between the Palestine Liberation Army and the Lebanese army. Syria responded by closing the border and although talks began in June, it was not until the 17th of August that it was reopened. The border closing was not attended by any drastic deterioration of relations and the Foreign Minister of Syria asserted that Syria had no desire to bring down the Lebanese regime, but that it only wished to help end the fighting. The Syrian government had, in fact, intervened with the Palestinians at one point for the release of Lebanese customs officials held by the guerrillas.

Following the reopening of the border, meetings and messages were commonplace at the highest levels, and on June 3, 1974 Syrian Foreign Minister Khaddam noted that Syrian-Lebanese relations were solidly based. By the end of 1974, Syria had not only offered to support Lebanon against attacks by Israel, which were launched in retaliation for Palestinian activities but it also promised to supply Lebanon with military aid. It is against this background of often fluctuating but currently cordial relations between Syria and Lebanon that the current struggle in Lebanon must be viewed.

"Greater Syria": Reviving an Old Concept

By DANIEL DISHON

President Assad of Syria has, since the beginning of 1975, begun to revive the concept of "Greater Syria." This concept was very current in the late 1940s and early 1950s. Syria, Lebanon, Jordan and Palestine were all to form one single geographical and political unit. The popularity of this idea stemmed largely from the fact that none of the four countries which constitute this area in their present borders has historical roots in Arab history. Each of these countries was created as a result of agreements made by the colonial powers—most particularly by Britain and France, after World War I. Arabs feel that these agreements, made by outside powers, no longer have political significance for them and that they therefore have no need to respect these entities or to think of them as realistically delineating the borders of viable Arab states.

In the 1940s and 1950s the idea of Greater Syria was one projected by the Hashemite dynasty in Jordan. Until 1945, this idea aimed at preventing Syria from becoming independent: Syria was to be drawn into a new, enlarged Hashemite Kingdom the moment the French departed. The Hashemite dynasty in Jordan was to move to Damascus, where their kingdom had originally been

Dr. Dishon is a Senior Research Member of the Shiloah Center for Middle Eastern and African Studies at Tel Aviv University and editor of the Center's *Middle East Record*.

proclaimed immediately after World War I. They would then reorganize this area to form the Kingdom of Greater Syria, under Hashemite rule.

It is one of the ironies of Middle East history that the revival of the Greater Syria concept is now one which has been initiated in republican Damascus—and from the point of view of a military leftist ideological leader—and that it would eventually, if actually carried out, probably mean that Syria would swallow Jordan rather than that the Hashemites of Jordan would swallow Syria.

In the late 1950s and throughout the 1960s, the Greater Syria idea became dormant, because political realities were such that neither party was strong enough to realize it; this idea has now taken on new significance.

In Jordan King Abdallah had actually made it official Jordanian policy to strive for a Greater Syria under Hashemite rule. This would next in some fashion be linked up with Iraq, which was then also under Hashemite rule; there would be some kind of federation between the two Hashemite states. The Iraqis themselves had originally been thinking in terms of a larger unit. Since they were at the time the stronger branch of the Hashemite dynasty, they thought in terms of the ''Fertile Crescent,'' to consist of Greater Syria and Iraq, to be run from Iraq rather than from Damascus and to be ruled by the Iraqi branch of the Hashemite family.

King Abdallah was the primary force behind the Greater Syria idea and although after his death in 1952 it became dormant as a program for political action, it did not die out as a political concept. The Syrians suggested it on many occasions. At the time of the Six Day War, they evoked it by referring to Palestine (and not for the first time) as Southern Syria. Jordan, or at least northern Jordan (the area of Irbid) was also usually considered Southern Syria by the Syrians and Jordan's population has a clear division of loyalties and lifestyles—people in the area north of Amman tend to look to Damascus as their center and feel more akin to the Syrians than do people in the area of Amman itself and further south. During the invasion of Jordan by the Syrians in 1970 it was precisely this element of the Jordanian population that the Syrians hoped to exploit. They did not succeed, but the idea was certainly there.

The concept is now being revived in the light of the Syrian-Egyptian rift following the latter's interim disengagement agreement with Israel and the political disintegration of Lebanon. Assad, who has been in power longer than any other president of an independent Syria, and who feels the need to make his mark against Egypt—because of the feeling that the Egyptians are working in their own interests and forgetting about Syrian interests—has a renewed motivation to do so.

The first signal was Assad's visit to Beirut in January 1975. Syria has never recognized the separate existence of Lebanon. There have been contacts, but never diplomatic relations. The Syrians have always taken the view that Lebanon was carved out of Syrian territory at the end of the French mandatory period as a sort of parting shot on the part of the French in order to hurt Syria.

Through the succeeding ten months it can be seen that Assad concentrated on precisely this idea—the historical outline of ''Greater Syria.'' There was the rapprochement with Jordan reaching its peak in the establishment of a Supreme Coordinating Committee—a body that may not be of great importance in itself but that is certainly an indication that both countries regard themselves as having moved very close indeed. Then there was the proposal made by Assad in March of 1975 to form a joint political and military command with the Palestinians which, baldly, was a Syrian bid to take over the PLO and make it an appendage of Syrian policy. The PLO did not fail to take note of the fact that this was a thinly-disguised takeover attempt and have been dragging their feet ever since. They have discussed it time and again and have asked for extra clarification; they know what they are up against.

In Lebanon, the main Syrian interest has been to make Syria indispensable in Lebanese affairs. This was achieved partly by establishing very clearly in Beirut that it is in Syria's power to put the whole problem on a back burner or on a front burner—to influence the PLO or at least al-Sa'iqa, which is the second largest body within the PLO and is run by Syria, in such a way that street fighting could flare up according to a pattern set from Damascus; and partly by making it clear to the President of Lebanon that major appointments need some kind of clearance from Damascus. In early 1975, for instance, the Lebanese had to accept Karami as Prime Minister against the opposition of his own President but with pressure from Syria. Later on, when Karami wanted to resign, the first thing he did was to go to Damascus to discuss it with Assad. Assad must have said no, because Karami did not tender his resignation. But the important point is that a politician wants to hand in his own resignation to his own President and goes to Damascus first to find out whether he should or should not. This is exactly what the Syrians have in mind. They want to make it clear for the future where the real power lies.

Next time around the Syrians will try to get Iraq involved as well. They will try to get rid of the hostile Iraqi Ba'th party (which they are trying to subvert) and if they can do that they will revive an even older and perhaps even more potent idea, that of the Fertile Crescent, which is Greater Syria plus Iraq.

But ''Greater Syria'' is today still only a concept by way of a contingency plan. The Syrians are not thinking in terms of an institutionalized merger or a merger of states as happened between Syria and Egypt in 1958. This has gone out of fashion and suggests unpleasant memories of the 1950s and 1960s. However, they would like to produce a situation in which Damascus is the place to which both Jordan and Lebanon, as well as the PLO have to turn in order to clear major decisions. In this geographical area, they feel, no major event should be allowed to happen unless and until it is cleared with Damascus. The Syrians may not quite have made up their minds yet to follow the Greater Syria plan, but that seems to be the basic pattern they are following.

Lebanon, the Soviet Union and the Syrian-PLO-Jordanian Entente

By ROBERT O. FREEDMAN

Developments in the Middle East in 1975 have led a number of observers to contend that a Greater Syria composed of Syria, Jordan and a Syrian and Palestinian-dominated Lebanon was being created with active Soviet encouragement and would become a center of pro-Soviet activity in the Middle East. These developments have included Syria's offer of a "Joint Command" to the Palestine Liberation Organization, Syria's economic and political rapprochement with its erstwhile Arab enemy, Jordan, and Syrian intervention in the Lebanese civil war on the side of Palestinian and Muslim forces. In each case, the Soviet Union offered its encouragement, evidently hoping that the three developments would not only strengthen the position of the PLO and Syria, two of the USSR's main Middle Eastern allies, but also detach Lebanon and Jordan from the pro-Western camp of Arab states.

The background for Syria's Middle Eastern moves over the past year lies in the Kissinger disengagement shuttle in the Spring of 1975. Despite the ultimate failure of the Spring shuttle, there was a great deal of concern expressed by Syria, the PLO and the Soviet Union that Egypt would sign a second disengagement pact with Israel (as indeed it was ultimately to do in August). It was feared that this would leave Syria isolated as the primary confrontation state facing Israel, with the PLO in a similarly weakened position—particularly at a time when Christian politicians in Lebanon such as Pierre Gemayel were openly calling for the ouster of Palestinian forces from Lebanese soil and the battles between Christian and Palestinian forces were beginning to take place. Given the continued bitter relations between Israel and Syria—Israel was complaining about Syrian maltreatment of Israeli prisoners of war and Syria was complaining about the destruction of the city of Quneitra—it appeared unlikely that Israel would sign any interim agreements with Syria, if only because there was not sufficient room to make anything more than a "cosmetic" change in the Israeli defensive positions. Consequently, it appeared that any settlement dealing with the Golan Heights would come only in the context of a final peace settlement between Israel and Syria. Movement toward such a settlement had reached an impasse because of Syrian demands—which Israel had rejected—that the PLO should be seated as an equal member at the Geneva peace talks. It should also be

Dr. Freedman is the Dean of Peggy Meyerhoff Pearlstone School of Graduate Studies, Baltimore Hebrew College and the author of *Economic Warfare in the Communist Bloc: A Study of Soviet Economic Pressure Against Yugoslavia, Albania, and Communist China* (New York: Praeger, 1970) and *Soviet Policy Toward the Middle East Since 1970* (New York: Praeger, 1975).

remembered that Syria had come under severe Palestinian criticism for its disengagement agreement with Israel in May 1974 and that one factor helping President Assad to gain legitimacy from his largely Sunni Muslim population was his support of the Palestinian cause. Thus Assad had a number of reasons for his offer of a "Joint Command" to the Palestinians. It would strengthen his internal position while also insuring that Syria would not be isolated against Israel, whatever Egypt did. It also meant, however, that the loosely federated PLO would be subordinated to Syria, and this factor made the Palestinian leaders hesitate to accept the Syrian offer.

Jordan's turn toward Syria was also aimed at averting Jordanian isolation in the event of an Egyptian-Israeli disengagement agreement. Syrian-Jordanian relations had hit their lowest point in September 1970 when Salah J'did, then Syria's leader, dispatched a tank force to aid the Palestinians in their life-and-death struggle with the Jordanian army. Following the failure of this move, J'did was replaced by Assad, although King Hussein's pressure against the Palestinians kept Syrian-Jordanian relations tense. Indeed, Assad closed the Syrian border to Jordanian goods on several occasions in protest against the king's actions, causing, thereby, serious damage to the Jordanian economy. Relations between the two countries did improve, however, after 1972 and reached a new point of cooperation when King Hussein dispatched a Jordanian tank force to aid the hard-pressed Syrian forces during the latter part of the 1973 Arab-Israeli war. Consequently, the March 1975 Jordanian-Syrian agreement, which was economic in nature but with strong political overtones, can be seen both as a climax to the improvement of relations between the two countries and, from the Syrian viewpoint, a means to strengthen Syria's southern flank in the face of an Israeli-Egyptian agreement.

King Hussein's motives for entering into this and two other agreements with Syria in June and August 1975 would appear to be considerably more complex. In the first place, an improved relationship with Assad would strengthen Hussein's position against the PLO which had not foresaken its pledge to overthrow him but which depended on Syria for most of its support— particularly since the outbreak of hostilities in Lebanon. Consequently, in return for close cooperation with Jordan, Hussein may well have extracted a pledge from Assad to keep the PLO under tight control and to prevent any covert or overt actions against his regime. Secondly, the economic agreements with Syria would be a major boon to the Jordanian economy and would deter Syria from again closing its border to Jordanian commerce. Thirdly, the agreements served to strengthen Hussein's bargaining position both against Israel and against the United States, since it also removed Jordan from a position of isolation. Jordan was moving toward a large arms purchase from the United States and the Jordanian gesture toward Syria may have been expected to be seen in Washington as a first step toward procuring arms from the USSR. Hussein, therefore, may have expected Kissinger to promise him virtually all the arms he wanted—as indeed Kissinger did—although if this was one of Hussein's purposes in moving closer to Syria he failed to consider the increasing power of the U.S. Congress in world affairs: it vetoed a large part of the arms agreement Kissinger had worked out, and substantial changes in the arms agreement had to be made before Congress would accept it.

While both Syria and Jordan, therefore, had reasons to draw together as Kissinger continued his shuttle diplomacy between Egypt and Israel, Syria also had to be concerned about the virtual civil war that had erupted in Lebanon by early Fall, with Christian forces fighting Muslims and Palestinians. While Syria was not averse to weakening the Christian elite which controlled the key positions of power in Lebanon, it was concerned about the aid that was being funnelled to left-wing Muslim forces by Libya and Iraq, two of Syria's Arab enemies. The aid from Iraq was of particular concern to the Syrian government, which was locked in a bitter conflict with the rival Ba'thist regime in Baghdad. Syria's fear was that if left-wing elements allied with Iraq were to come to power in Lebanon, Syria would find itself sandwiched between two unfriendly Arab regimes—and also have to face Israel. Consequently, as the civil war in Lebanon became more intense, Syrian intervention became more and more open until the Syrian government finally dispatched a Palestinian army force under Syrian command to restore order. The Syrian intervention was, at least initially, successful. In early February, 1976, it appeared that a Pax Syriana had been imposed on Lebanon's warring factions, although the ultimate aim of the Syrian government's policy remained unclear.

What can be said of the Soviet role in these Middle Eastern events? Since the October 1973 war, the Soviet Union has been competing for influence with a resurgent United States which, despite Watergate, a severe recession and losses in Southeast Asia, had nonetheless been able to improve its position in the Middle East through Kissinger's successful negotiation of the series of disengagement agreements. Seeing the Arab states of the Middle East as a kind of zero-sum game arena for superpower competition, where what one superpower gains the other must lose, the Russians have viewed with alarm Egypt's move into the American camp and have feared a similar move by other Soviet allies, including Iraq and Syria. To prevent such a development, the Soviet leadership has sought to establish an "anti-imperialist" Arab unity whereby the Arab states would rally to the Soviet side in opposition to the "imperialist West" and its Middle East ally, Israel. The USSR, however, has encountered a considerable amount of difficulty in creating this "anti-imperialist Arab unity," because of the intense interstate and intra-state rivalries that plague the Arab world—although it came close to its goal during the 1973 Arab-Israeli war when virtually the entire Arab world was aligned against Israel and the United States. Unfortunately for the Soviet leadership, however, the anti-imperialist Arab unity they had so warmly welcomed did not survive the war, as Egypt began to move toward the United States and Libya and Iraq rejected Soviet peace initiatives. In addition, Iraq and Syria entered into conflict over water from the Euphrates Dam and other issues and Morocco and Algeria battled over the former Spanish Sahara. Meanwhile, as Kissinger scored success after success in his disengagement efforts, the Russians were hard put to reverse the pro-American trend that appeared to be emerging in the Middle East. Consequently, the Soviet leadership saw the Syrian-Jordanian rapprochement as a vehicle to both isolate Sadat in the Arab world—thereby weakening U.S. peace efforts—and also to draw Jordan away from its tie to the United States. The Syrian-PLO alignment was to serve to protect the Palestinian forces in Lebanon against "reactionary" attempts to destroy them, thus preserving one of the constituent elements of the "anti-imperialist" Arab unity the Russians were trying to build. Indeed, the USSR supported the Syrian intervention in Lebanon for this reason and also because of the possibility that Lebanon might thereby be detached from the pro-Western grouping of Arab states.

Nonetheless, the outcome of these Syrian moves may not prove totally beneficial to the USSR, and they do not necessarily herald the emergence of a "Greater Syria." Indeed, if a lasting Pax Syriana is imposed on Lebanon—and this is beginning to appear unlikely—both Soviet and PLO interests may suffer. The PLO is tightly controlled in Syria and its fate may be the same in a Syrian-dominated Lebanon—a factor that would lead to hostility between the PLO and Syria, particularly if Assad is serious about his tie with Hussein. Similarly, Assad has kept the Syrian Communist Party under tight control and he might do the same in Lebanon, thereby depriving the Soviet Union of a major propaganda outlet in the Arab world.

All in all, therefore, given the continued conflict between King Hussein and the PLO, and the potential for conflict between Syria and the PLO in a Syrian-dominated Lebanon—to say nothing of the difficulties the Syrians will encounter as they try to control the disparate elements in Lebanon—it would appear that the establishment of a Greater Syria is still a very long way off and that the USSR may itself not be totally in favor of such a development.

V

Syria and the Soviet Union

The History of Soviet Intervention in Syria

By YAACOV RO'I

From the early 1950s two Arab states attracted Soviet attention as potential allies: Syria and Egypt. Both these states had a deep commitment to hostility to the West, which the Soviet Union correctly interpreted as providing a promising basis for cooperation in undermining the Western monopoly of influence and power in the Arab world.

In 1950 Moscow was already putting out feelers for an economic aid agreement with Syria that was to include the supply of military materiel. However, conditions only became ripe for a meaningful dialogue between the two states with the fall of the pro-Western Syrian dictator Adib Shishakli in 1954 and the concurrent preparations for what became the Baghdad Pact. This military alliance brought the "northern tier" states (Turkey, Iraq, Iran and Pakistan) together with Britain and the United States into a regional treaty directed primarily against the Soviet Union, but which Syria—like Egypt—considered a threat to its own sovereignty. This created a convergence of interests between Damascus and Moscow that led to military and economic agreements as well as political collaboration in the Middle Eastern and international arenas. The Syrian-Israeli dispute over the demilitarized zones on their common border was the occasion for the earliest indication of this collaboration, in the form of the first Soviet veto in the Security Council in January 1954.

In 1957 the Soviet-Syrian rapprochement took on new dimensions. What first appeared as a difference of degree became one of substance, with the advancement on the Syrian domestic scene of both civilian and military groupings and individuals known for their pro-Soviet orientations. This was accompanied by the large-scale supply of military equipment generally considered to be far above the immediate absorption capacity of the Syrian armed forces and by a Soviet-exacerbated Syrian-Turkish crisis that became a major international issue in the Fall of 1957, with the Soviet Union accusing Turkey of preparing a Western-inspired invasion of Syria. The Soviet Union, however, overplayed its hand. Alarmed by growing Soviet domination, a number of Syrian public figures sought an alternative by approaching Egyptian President Abdel Nasser with the suggestion that the two states be federated. Thus, early in 1958, the United Arab Republic (U.A.R.) was established.

Dr. Ro'i is a member of The Russian and East European Research Center at Tel Aviv University, Israel. He is the author of *From Encroachment To Involvement: A Documentary Study of Soviet Policy in the Middle East, 1945-1973*, (Halsted Press, 1974).

In the ensuing period Soviet influence in Syria existed only as a function of the Soviet Union's relationship with Nasser, and earlier ties were not easily renewed after Syria's secession from the U.A.R. in September 1961 despite the Soviet Union's speedy recognition of the new Syrian regime. Yet, toward the end of 1963, the Syrian Ba'th Party, which had taken power that Spring, adopted a program that contained a large dose of Marxist-Leninist doctrine and terminology, preached a new "Arab road to socialism" and relegated the theory of Arab unity—which had been a serious obstacle to a Soviet rapprochement—to the background. The development—and particularly the implementation—of large-scale nationalization measures, which alienated Western economic connections, brought Syria increasingly into the Soviet orbit.

This trend was further enhanced by the February 1966 coup which brought the Ba'th's left wing to power. The increased radicalism of Salah J'did and his associates included decisions to cooperate with individual members of the Syrian Communist Party, who were coopted into the government, and also expansion of cooperation with the Soviet Union. This resulted not only in extensive Soviet military and economic aid programs, including the Euphrates Dam project—which was to be "a second Aswan"—but also, the Syrian Ba'th party's decision to model its organizational and institutional structure and its socialist experiment on those of the East European People's Democracies. This necessitated intensive contacts with virtually all levels of the relevant establishments in order to study their experience and adapt it to Syrian conditions and requirements. Finally, the new relationship involved unreserved Soviet support for Syria in the increasing tension that was building up in the Syrian-Israeli theater.

Indeed, the worsening situation with Israel gave a new operational significance to Soviet military aid to Syria. In addition to the actual supply of arms, Soviet experts were training and advising the Syrian army in logistics, intelligence procedures and the handling and maintenance of equipment. Some of these Soviet officers were attached to the southwestern front headquarters at Quneitra. The importance ascribed by the Soviet Union to Syria at the time was manifested in the pressures it applied to prevent Israel from opening up the Golan Heights front in June 1967 and, once fighting had begun there, to put a speedy end to hostilities.

After the Six Day War, Egypt (still officially the U.A.R.) was the main focus of Soviet attention in the Arab world, although political contacts with Syria—on both the party and the government level—continued unabated, as did economic and military aid, the latter including the speedy replenishment of equipment lost in the war. The main reasons for Syria's secondary position as the 1960s drew to a close derived largely from the special Soviet relationship with Nasser and partly also from the Syrian rejection of political methods of "liquidating the consequences of the aggression" and of Security Council Resolution 242 of November 22, 1967.

With the death of Nasser, however, and the Soviet Union's increasing difficulties in its relations with Sadat's Egypt, Moscow again drew close to Syria. The overthrow of J'did and the advent to power of Hafez al-Assad in November 1970 in no way impaired the new rapprochement, although Assad was not considered one of the Soviet Union's traditional supporters in the Syrian leadership. It is true that the new President resisted Soviet attempts to conclude a friendship and cooperation treaty with Syria on the lines of the treaties signed with Egypt in 1971 and Iraq in 1972, yet he accepted the necessity for his country's pro-Soviet orientation and maintained constant ties with the Kremlin. Moreover, he made an important concession, which J'did had consistently resisted, by agreeing in 1972 to set up a national front of the country's "progressive" groupings, thus enabling the Communist party as such to become an official part of the establishment, although the Ba'th retained actual power.

The Soviet-Syrian relationship played a major role in smoothing over difficulties between the Soviet Union and Egypt in the period after the July 1972 crisis, when Assad acted as mediator between his two allies. In the wake of the October 1973 Yom Kippur War, however, the ties between Syria and the Soviet Union became even more crucial to both partners. Egypt's increasing connections with the U.S. made the Soviet Union lean more and more heavily on its links with Syria, the second major confrontation state, in order to ensure its own participation in the negotiating process. Furthermore, Sadat's willingness to enter into separate bilateral agreements with Israel made Syria increasingly reliant on Soviet support to help Syria achieve minimal terms—as seen from Damascus—in the same process. Because of this mutual interest the Soviet Union not only speedily replenished the war materiel Syria had lost in October 1973 but also supplemented this equipment with what Moscow has traditionally termed "offensive arms," including two squadrons of Mig-23s and Scud ground-to-ground missiles.

Syria's successes in inter-Arab politics, notably its new relationship with Jordan and its *modus vivendi* with the Palestinian organizations, and Syrian leverage regarding developments in Lebanon (on whose precarious status quo the Russians have long had an eye) have enhanced Syria's value in Moscow. At the same time, however, the Soviet Union's complete inability to contribute to the settlement process (let alone on the lines that Syria desires) seems to have evoked some reevaluation in Damascus of Syria's special relationship with the Soviet Union. At present this reassessment appears to contain the seeds of a more pro-American policy.

As yet, however, the Soviet Union still has a very extensive presence in Syria with deep roots in that country's polity, armed forces and economy. The affinity of socio-political aspirations has meant that Moscow, besides serving as a model, continues to maintain a plethora of contacts with the Syrian party and government establishment at various levels. Military aid has brought

Soviet military advisers to all branches and levels of the Syrian armed forces and has given the Soviet Union access to all Syria's military and strategic secrets, its facilities in Lataqia and Tartus, obvious operational leverage on Syrian tactics in the field and even a hand in strategic planning. Economic aid, based on the usual Soviet criteria of constructing show enterprises and boosting the primary sectors of the national economy—such as transport, agriculture, oil-prospecting and drilling—has brought Soviet economic personnel to the remotest corners of the country and has enabled them to pervade and exercise some control over the most vital spheres of the country's economy. Finally, political cooperation in the international arena on both regional and global levels, particularly the Soviet Union's largely unrestrained animosity toward Israel, has enabled both Syria and the Soviet Union to reap mutual benefit from a policy of relative extremism that has widened the rift between Syria and Egypt and is obviously hindering any Syrian rapprochement with Washington. Although the latter is not impossible, the Soviet Union seems to be striving hard to make itself valuable, if not irreplaceable, to its most important remaining partner in the Arab world.

The Soviet-Syrian Military Aid Relationship

By ROGER F. PAJAK

In the Soviet drive to establish a presence and gain influence in the Middle East, military assistance has clearly emerged as Moscow's most durable and effective instrument of policy. The priority accorded the Middle East in Soviet foreign policy calculations is reflected in the share of total Soviet arms aid allocated to the area. Of the estimated $12 billion in such assistance extended to the nonaligned, developing countries of the Third World from 1955 through 1974, the Arab states of the Middle East have received about $7 billion, or roughly 60 percent of the total.[1]

While Egypt has served as the linchpin of Soviet Middle Eastern policy for the past two decades, Syria concomitantly has been integral to Moscow's interests in the area. Moreover, given the severely strained Soviet relationship with Cairo of late, Soviet interests in Damascus have recently become all the more acute.

Dr. Pajak is a Foreign Adviser with the U.S. Arms Control and Disarmament Agency, serving as political specialist on Soviet-Middle East Affairs, the Arab-Israeli military situation and the international arms trade. He has written extensively on Soviet policy in the Middle East.

The above has been updated by the author and is adapted from his article entitled ''Soviet Military Aid to Iraq and Syria'' which appeared in *Strategic Review,* Vol. IV, No. 1, Winter 1976, by permission of *Strategic Review.*

With $2.1 billion in Soviet military assistance received through 1974, Syria ranks next to Egypt as the largest recipient of Soviet arms among the nonaligned countries.[2] Soviet military cooperation with Syria dates from 1956, when in January of that year, the Syrian government concluded its first arms accord with Moscow, because of the "impossible conditions" for purchasing arms attached by the West. After the 1956 accord, follow-on agreements, technical assistance, and goodwill naval visits followed in the usual Soviet pattern.[3]

Though encountering problems and periodic setbacks, a Soviet working relationship was maintained with Syria over the next decade. By the eve of the June 1967 War, Syrian military and economic dependence on Moscow was pronounced.[4]

Though not suffering as heavily in the June War as Egypt, Syrian equipment losses were substantial. In aircraft, for example, Syria lost thirty-two MIG-21s, twenty-three MIG-15/17s, two IL-28 bombers, and three helicopters, for a total of sixty aircraft, or practically two-thirds of her entire air force.[5]

Within a year, however, Soviet resupply had more than replaced Syria's losses. Replacement deliveries, reportedly valued at about $300 million, included 120 aircraft—many late model MIG-21 and SU-7 fighters among them to replace earlier vintage MIG-15s and 17s lost in the conflict—and some 400 tanks. As many as 1,000 additional Soviet advisory personnel also arrived in the country. At the same time, Soviet long-range bombers initiated visits to Syria, and the construction of naval support facilities began under Soviet supervision in the ports of Lataqia and Tartous. The latter would prove valuable for Syrian naval craft as well as ships of the Soviet Mediterranean squadron, as regular Soviet naval visits in 1968 began to demonstrate.[6]

While Syria remained crucial to Soviet calculations in the area, policy differences between the two countries grew more acute after the June War. The apparent central difference was over policy toward Israel. In contrast to Moscow's espousal of a political approach to a settlement, the Syrians continued to press for reprisals and the total defeat of Israel, as underscored by their heavy support of the Palestinian guerrillas. These differences placed a considerable strain on Soviet-Syria relations.[7]

At the end of 1968, reports in the Lebanese press mentioned Syrian attempts to approach the West for military equipment, ostensibly because of Soviet threats to withhold arms if Damascus continued to oppose an Arab-Israeli political settlement. Although a Syrian military delegation returned empty-handed from Paris, Damascus shortly afterwards concluded a new agreement with Moscow, in an apparent successful use of counterpressure on the Soviets.[8]

The Syrians apparently tried to repeat this tactic the following year, when in May 1969, General Tlas headed a mission to Peking. The aim reportedly was to pressure the Soviets to provide additional advanced weapons by seeking assistance from the Chinese.[9] The latter turned down a reported Syrian request for SAMs, but did agree to provide infantry weapons for the Palestinian guerrillas based in Syria.[10]

By the middle of 1970, three years after the June War, Syria was nearly totally dependent on the Soviet Union for the sustenance of its military machine. The air force, which had tripled in size since the war, boasted 175 late-model MIG-21 fighters and SU-7 fighter bombers (as opposed to fifty-five before the war) and eighty-five MIG-17 fighters.[11] Deliveries to the ground forces during the three year period included 250-300 tanks, over 100 armored personnel carriers, 400 field guns and mobile rocket launchers, and an estimated forty SA-2 SAM missiles.[12] Transfers to the navy included two Soviet-supplied minesweepers, six *Komar*-class missile patrol boats, and at least a dozen motor torpedo boats.[13]

Striving to correct the operational deficiencies in the Syrian armed forces were an estimated 2,000 to 3,000 Soviet military instructors and advisers, perhaps one-fifth the number in Egypt at the time. As in Egypt the Soviet personnel were engaged in training, planning, and logistics activities down to divisional, and in some cases lower, levels. Although some improvement was said to have been made in Syrian-operational efficiency since the June War, Soviet officers in Syria did not consider the Syrian forces ready for renewed hostilities with Israel. [14] Operational and maintenance standards remained lamentably poor, a partial legacy of the eight coups d'etat undergone by the country in the previous seventeen years. Morale in the armed forces accordingly remained at a low ebb.[15]

Another military aid agreement signed with Moscow in February 1971 continued the flow of materiel in that year. Deliveries over the next six months included thirty-five additional fighter aircraft and twenty-two MI-8 helicopters—the first known delivery of the latter craft, designed to carry combat troops.[16]

While the April 1972 Soviet friendship treaty with Iraq received considerable attention in the Western press, conspicuous by its absence was a similar treaty with Syria. Surprisingly enough, Syrian wariness over a closer involvement with Moscow reportedly caused Damascus to reject a Soviet offer of such a treaty.[17] Another Soviet-Syrian arms accord, however, was signed in May, the accord promising the Syrians their first SA-3 SAMs, as well as additional missile-equipped patrol boats.[18]

Following the sudden ouster of virtually all Soviet personnel from Egypt in July 1972, Western observers awaited some reactive move by the Soviets in the area. It came two months later in the form of a prominent airlift of Soviet military equipment to Syria. During late September and early October, some twenty AN-12 transport aircraft, as well as several merchant ships, arrived in Syria with new equipment, reportedly including twelve to fifteen MIG-21 fighters, new T-62 medium tanks, and SA-3 missiles.[19] Also arriving in the airlift were a reported 150 new Soviet advisers, possibly SA-3 instructors and technicians, adding to the several thousand already in the country.[20] Moscow evidently took this conspicuous and dramatic step to demonstrate that it still maintained a secure foothold in the Middle East.

Also in September, Western sources reported that Moscow negotiated some type of arrangement with Damascus, whereby the Soviets would expand naval facilities at the Syrian ports of Lataqia and Tartous for their use. Up to that time Soviet naval craft could only make port calls at those locations. The exact nature of the arrangement was not made clear, but the Soviets presumably planned to establish an alternate base of operations in the eastern Mediterranean, until the status of their Egyptian bases became clarified.[21]

The chief of Israeli military intelligence, General A. Yariv, publicly stated at the time that the Soviets were "playing up" developments in Syria to diplomatically bolster their position in the area following their setback in Egypt. While stating that Israel "must watch it carefully," Yariv commented that there were no signs of a substantial increase in the Soviet presence in the country—a factor of more concern to Israel than new equipment deliveries. He added that the recent shipments apparently were intended to bolster Syria's "relatively weak side," her air defense, given reports of the newly arrived SA-3 equipment.[22]

The diplomatic reaction from the September-October air and sealift had just abated, when another, even larger airlift began in November and continued into December. The latter, about twice as large as the previous airlift, involved about forty aircraft, including the very large AN-22 transport, capable of carrying a 220,000 pound payload. All that has been reported on the contents of the later airlift was the inclusion of an unspecified number of MIG-21 fighters, presumably to replace the dozen or more shot down in dogfights with the Israelis over the previous half year.[23]

Deliveries continued on a heavy scale during 1973. During the first six months, Soviet shipments amounted to a reported $185 million, compared with about $150 million for all of 1972.[24]

In September 1973, Syrian and Israeli aircraft tangled in the biggest air battle in the Middle East since the 1967 War. Israel claimed it shot down thirteen Syrian MIG-21s for the loss of one of its Mirages. The day following the battle, Soviet Ambassador Mukhitdinov was reportedly summoned by President Assad, who demanded advanced MIG-23 fighters from Moscow, as well as Soviet participation in Syrian SAM launch operations in future clashes with the Israelis. When the Soviets apparently demurred unless Damascus signed a friendship treaty with Moscow, Assad restricted the movement of Soviet advisers in the country.[25] "Those damned Syrians," complained Ambassador Mukhitdinov, "will take anything except advice."[26]

The October War showed the extent of the vast Soviet-supplied arsenal in Syria. The Syrians deployed a reported total of thirty-two SA-6 batteries (Egypt deployed forty-six), each battery having four launchers with three missiles apiece. In the first three days of hostilities, the number of SAM missiles fired on the combined Syrian and Egyptian fronts reportedly totalled over 1,000, reflecting a deployment density surpassing that of any known SAM system in the world, the Soviet Union included.[27] Syrian losses reportedly totalled 222 aircraft of all types (about two-thirds of total air force strength), some 1,100 tanks (50 per cent of total tank holdings), and 17-20 SAM batteries (over half of Syria's inventory).[28]

While Soviet arms deliveries to Egypt virtually ceased after the war, Soviet shipments to Syria continued at a high rate. By August 1974, Israeli Defense Minister Shimon Peres claimed that not only were Syrian losses replaced, but that Syria was stronger than before the war. Mr. Peres stated that Syrian air force strength totalled about 400 aircraft—about 25 per cent more than prior to October 1973—and that its SAM system was about 20 per cent larger. In addition, all tank losses had been made up, mostly with modern T-62s. Peres added that about 3,000 Soviet advisers were in Syria, some operating the missile defense system and other electronic equipment.[29] A Pentagon spokesman in effect subsequently confirmed the Israeli information, saying he would not quarrel with the levels mentioned by Peres. He added, however, that U.S. analysts estimated the number of Soviet advisers present at about 2,000.[30]

Besides replacing Syrian war losses, the Soviets provided additional modern equipment to Damascus. In the spring of 1974, the first advanced swing-wing MIG-23 fighters were identified in Syria, the first country outside the Soviet Union to receive this late-model aircraft. A total of forty-five M-23s were reported in the country.[31] Other newly arrived sophisticated equipment included 30 *Scud* surface-to-surface missiles with a range of 180 miles, over 100 *Frog* shorter-range tactical rockets,[32] vehicle-mounted multiple SA-7 SAM launchers, and new 180 mm howitzers.[33] The *Scuds*, with their capability of striking Israeli cities with high explosive warheads, posed the gravest concern to Tel Aviv and raised the threat of an Israeli pre-emptive strike in the event of an imminent renewal of hostilities.[34]

Prior to the post-October resupply of the Syrians, Israeli military planning was based on the premise that Egypt was the fulcrum of war or peace in the area. It was further regarded that no war was feasible without Egyptian participation, and that while Cairo was involved in negotiations, the likelihood of hostilities was not imminent.[35]

The spate of Soviet shipments to Syria in 1974 changed the outlook of the Israelis. The latter by mid-year regarded the Syrians as capable of launching a full-scale onslaught on their own, with the expectation that the Iraqis and other Arab countries would join in.[36] Indeed, U.S. officials at that time also felt that "the Syrians were well ahead of where they were before the war," as a result of the heavy volume of Soviet deliveries, while the Egyptians were approximately at their prewar strength. Concomitantly, Washington regarded Israel as stronger militarily vis-à-vis both Egypt and Syria than before the war.[37]

The critical Syrian weakness remained trained and experienced manpower. Half of Syria's tanks were reportedly manned by inexperienced crews, while many aircraft remained grounded due to the shortage of fully qualified pilots, only about sixty of whom were reported to have survived the war.[38] Until

Syrian pilots could be trained, some of the newly arrived MIG-23s were reportedly being flown by Cuban and North Korean pilots.[39]

The presence of the North Korean and Cuban contingents dates from the October 1973 war. According to Arab sources, North Korean pilots flew defensive operational missions for the Syrians during the war. Some North Korean casualties were reported, but no reliable figures were available.[40]

To further strengthen the Syrian forces, the Soviets reportedly concluded a major new arms agreement in October 1975, during the visit to Moscow of Syrian President Assad. While details were sketchy, the arrangement was said to call for the provision of 500 additional tanks of the T-55 variety over a two year period. This would amount to a 25 percent increase in the existing Syrian inventory of 2,100 tanks, according to Israeli officials.[41] The deal also was reported to include additional advanced aircraft and surface-to-air missiles.[42]

At about the same time, the Soviets reportedly were negotiating with the Syrians for the use of an air base to station several MIG-25 *Foxbat* reconnaissance aircraft. Four of these Soviet-manned high performance aircraft, among the most advanced in the Soviet inventory, had been operating in Egypt until September 1975, when Soviet-Egyptian strains resulted in their withdrawal.[43] Their primary purpose reportedly was surveillance of US naval activities in the eastern Mediterranean. Israeli officials stated that several *Foxbats*—presumably piloted by Soviets—had arrived in Syria by November 1975.[44]

Even as the Soviet arms aid relationship remained active, however, Damascus in the fall of 1975 concluded its first sizable arms accord with a non-communist country in years in the form of a French deal for helicopters and antitank missiles. In October 1975 it was reported that France would provide Syria with at least 15 *Super Frelon* helicopters and some 2,000 antitank missiles, to be funded by Saudi Arabia.[45] The motivations for the purchase from France were not clear, but Syria may simply have taken advantage of a Saudi offer to procure some equipment for Syria from a non-communist source. It remains to be seen whether Syria, now subsidized by Saudi funds,[46] will continue its tentative probings toward the West for military equipment, or will remain closely tied to Moscow.

By the very nature of its contribution to the strengthening and survival of the Syrian regime, arms aid over the course of two decades has proven to be an extraordinarily impactful element of Soviet policy toward this Arab state. Fostering an image of the Soviet Union as a powerful friend and benefactor, the arms aid program has served as a prime instrument for acquiring influence in Syria, where Moscow's role otherwise would have been much more limited.

At the same time, the program has not proved to be an unmitigated blessing for Moscow. There is little, if any, evidence to suggest that arms aid has enabled the Soviets to exercise leverage for political concessions in Syria. Neither have the activities of the Syrian Communist Party been facilitated by the existence of the aid program. Moreover, Moscow has discovered that its material largesse has resulted in a variety of risks and problems. The ready provision of military equipment and training by Moscow has nurtured a virtually complete dependence on the part of Syria, implying a continual obligation for such assistance on the part of the Soviet Union. Thus, becoming identified to some degree with the policies and actions of a client state over which it has had little real control, Moscow has found the situation both embarrassing and dangerous.

Despite some setbacks and frustrations, however, the Soviet leaders on balance probably view their arms aid program as their most effective policy instrument vis-á-vis Syria. Although the net cost of military aid has risen appreciably since the early days of the program, when equipment could readily be drawn from surplus stocks, there is little doubt that arms exports have proven a worthwhile political instrument from Moscow's point of view. Recent vicissitudes in Soviet relations with Syria notwithstanding, it appears that Moscow will maintain an arms aid relationship with its Arab protégé. Damascus has no viable alternative for a continuing source of modern weaponry and spare parts, and Moscow has too much at stake to do otherwise.

NOTES

1. U.S. Department of State, *Communist States and Developing Countries: Aid and Trade in 1974* (Washington, February 1976), p. 30.

2. *Ibid.*

3. George Lenczowski, *Soviet Advances in the Middle East,* Washington: American Enterprise Institute for Public Policy Research, February 1972, p. 105.

4. Ibid., p. 123.

5. Ibid., p. 152.

6. A. Yodfat, "The USSR, Jordan, and Syria," *Mizan,* March-April 1969, p. 84.

7. Charles McLane, *Soviet-Middle East Relations,* London: Central Asian Research Center, 1973, p. 91.

8. Yodfat, "The USSR, Jordan, and Syria," op. cit., p. 88.

9. *New York Times,* May 18, 1969.

10. Honorable R. Lawrence Coughlin, *Congressional Record,* Washington: U.S. Congress, September 16, 1969, p. E7537.

11. *Aviation Week and Space Technology,* June 1, 1970, p. 16.

12. Lenczowski, op. cit., p. 152.

13. Wynfred Joshua, *Soviet Penetration into the Middle East,* New York: National Strategy Information Center, 1970, p. 20.

14. *Christian Science Monitor,* July 9, 1970.

15. Robert Jackson, *The Israeli Air Force Story,* London: Central Asian Research Center, 1973, p. 168.

16. *New York Times,* July 12, 1971.

17. *Strategic Survey 1972,* op. cit., p. 27.

18. R. M. Burrell, "Opportunities for the Kremlin's Drive East," *New Middle East,* July 1972, p. 13.

19. *Washington Post,* September 28, 1972.

20. *Washington Post,* October 6, 1972.

21. *New York Times,* September 14, 1972.

22. *Washington Post,* September 28, 1972.

23. *Washington Post,* January 10, 1973.

24. London Sunday Times Staff, *The Yom Kippur War,* New York: Doubleday, 1974, p. 72.

25. *Washington Post,* September 26, 1973.

26. London Sunday Times Staff, op. cit., p. 72.

27. London Sunday Times Staff, op. cit., p. 189.

28. *New York Times,* August 8, 1974.

29. Ibid.

30. *Defense/Space Daily,* December 19, 1974, p. 264.

31. *Washington Post,* September 12, 1974.

32. *Washington Post,* November 20, 1974.

33. *International Defense Review,* No. 3, May-June 1974, p. 284.

34. *Washington Post,* November 20, 1974.

35. *New York Times,* August 8, 1974.

36. Ibid.

37. *New York Times,* October 3, 1974.

38. *U.S. News and World Report,* March 17, 1975, p. 14.

39. *Time,* December 2, 1974, p. 46.

40. *Washington Post,* January 30, 1976.

41. *Baltimore Sun,* November 23, 1975.

42. *Defense and Foreign Affairs Daily,* October 30, 1975, p. 2.

43. *Baltimore Sun,* November 23, 1975.

44. *New York Times,* November 18, 1975.

45. *Washington Post,* October 17, 1975; *Defense and Foreign Affairs Daily,* October 30, 1975, p. 2.

46. *Washington Post,* June 23, 1975.

Soviets Expand Weapons Aid to Syria

By DREW MIDDLETON

Expanded deliveries of arms and munitions by the Soviet Union to Syria and an expected increase in the number of Russian military advisers there are causing concern among Israeli and United States military sources.

The acceleration of Soviet arms aid followed the visit to Moscow . . . [in October, 1975] of President Hafez al-Assad of Syria. After Mr. Assad's return to Damascus, Maj. Gen. Mustafa T'las, the Syrian Defense Minister, remained in the Soviet capital to work out the details of the military assistance program.

A key element of that program, the sources said, will be the reinforcement of the Soviet military adviser group. Its strength is now estimated at 3,500 officers, non-commissioned officers and technical experts.

Soviet intentions, as assessed by American and Western-European experts, are to establish Syria as the primary Arab military power, while Egypt seeks arms from the United States and in Western Europe. Moscow can thus demonstrate to other Arab nations that friendly governments can be certain of quick and extensive Soviet military aid.

The evaluation is that the Soviet Union is not ready to back Syrian military action against Israel on the Golan Heights, but that Moscow will continue to support an aggressive Syrian diplomatic position, demanding the return of all the territory occupied by Israel.

The overall assessment is that the Syrian staff believes that the army is sufficiently strong to defend Damascus against an Israeli thrust or, if necessary, make a limited attack on the forward Israeli positions on the Golan Heights.

Syria, in the words of one well-qualified source, is in a position "to institute a war of attrition, shelling and bombing, against the Israelis on the Heights." The prospects for an all-out offensive would depend on the attitude of Jordan and Iraq. The extent of Soviet arms aid to Syria is also causing concern over the possibility of Syrian intervention in Lebanon, if the fighting there continues.

Experts point out that a cardinal theme of Syrian nationalism is that Lebanon is a part of "Greater Syria."

The danger of Syrian intervention, Israeli sources said, is that Israel could not stand idly by and allow Syria to take strategically important areas on her northern frontier. The emphasis in Soviet arms aid to Syria, according to reports reaching other Middle Eastern capitals, is on advanced equipment. Soviet arms deliveries from December 1973 through March 1974 made up for the heavy Syrian tank losses in the October war of 1973.

Reprinted by permission of *The New York Times*, October 26, 1975.

Since then the Syrians have received 45 MIG-23s, the most advanced Soviet fighter deployed outside the Soviet Union, and approximately 75 MIG-21s, raising the interceptor force to around 300 aircraft, as well as 15 additional SU-7 ground attack planes. Soviet technical advisers are reported to have increased the efficiency of the Syrian air control organization and to have introduced modern techniques for cooperation among radar stations, interceptors and surface-to-air missiles in defense.

Although the table of organization for surface-to-air missiles has gone unchanged—24 batteries of SA-2 and SA-3 launchers and 14 batteries of SA-6 launchers—the number of missiles available has been increased.

Soviet shipments have also raised the level of the Syrian inventory of surface-to-surface missiles for anti-tank use, particularly the "Sagger," "Snapper" and "Swatter" weapons. The names are those given the arms by the North Atlantic Treaty Organization. Another major arms transfusion has been in the field of armored personnel carriers and the new BMP scout cars. In a less spectacular but important aspect of military aid, the Soviet Union has attempted to break down the rigidity of Syrian tactics.

A Syrian weakness during the 1973 war was the tendency to repeat attack patterns, employing the same mix of tanks, armored personnel carriers and infantry over the same avenues of approach. Soviet advisers, it is reported, stress tactical flexibility on the offensive and a greater use of artillery to support attacks.

Soviet advisers have also been instrumental in bolstering Syrian defenses on the plain southwest of Damascus; the static defenses of surface-to-air missiles and anti-tank ditches and missiles have been altered to provide greater opportunity for counterattack by Syrian forces.

Both the arms shipments and the instruction by Soviet advisers, according to Western reports, have increased the confidence of the Syrian army and air force.

The withdrawal of an Egyptian fighter squadron by President Sadat . . .[in September, 1975] did not lessen this confidence, the sources said.

ARMS TRADE BY COUNTRY BY YEAR 1963-1973

(Millions of dollars)

COUNTRY	YEAR	EXPORTS		IMPORTS	
		Current dollars	Constant 1972 dollars	Current dollars	Constant 1972 dollars
SYRIA	1963	0.	0.	35.0	47.7
	1964	0.	0.	16.0	21.5
	1965	0.	0.	10.0	13.2
	1966	0.	0.	15.0	19.2
	1967	0.	0.	58.0	72.1
	1968	0.	0.	40.0	47.8
	1969	0.	0.	48.0	54.7
	1970	1.0	1.1	61.0	65.9
	1971	0.	0.	110.0	113.7
	1972	0.	0.	163.0	163.0
	1973	0.	0.	724.0	685.6
Growth (Avg. Ann)		—	0.	—	37.57
Correl. COEF-R		—	0.	—	.65

Source: Table V. in World Military Expenditures and Arms Trade, 1963-1973, U.S. Arms and Disarmament Agency, Washington, D.C. 20451.

The Transfer of Weapons to Syria

The Syrian military capacity has been vastly expanded and strengthened with Soviet arms. The following are among the equipment received:

Nov. 17, 1973: According to *Aviation Week,* a Soviet airborne division was transferred to Belgrade, Yugoslavia, while its command headquarters was relocated to Damascus. 60,000 tons of military supplies had gone through Rijeka, Yugoslavia every week, with no sign of a let up, since the October war.

Nov. 23, 1973: The *Baltimore Sun* reported that Pentagon experts believed that some 700 Soviet made T-62 tanks and 150 T-54s and T-55s had been sent to Syria since the war. Large quantities of heavy ground-to-ground Frog rockets were sent. Some 3,000 Soviet advisers and technicians were stationed in Syria.

Nov. 10, 1973: The *New York Times* reported that in addition to the Soviet arms, Western radar and sophisticated air defense equipment was being bought by Syria in large quantities. "The Syrians," the report stated, "appear to be offering cash in convertible Western currencies which is reportedly being provided by oil-rich Arab states such as Saudi Arabia and Kuwait."

Feb. 7, 1974: *Associated Press* reported that Soviet efforts in Syria were concentrated on rebuilding the Syrian Air Force. At least 7 MIG-21 jet fighters and other planes had arrived in Lataqia harbor as part of an overall shipment of some 130 Soviet planes to replace the 185 planes lost during the war. Shipments also included a missile boat and 9 KA-25 helicopters. Three new airfields were being completed. London reports said that Syria had rebuilt its Soviet-controlled missile defenses.

Feb. 25, 1974: The French weekly, *L'Express,* reported that SAM-3 and SAM-6 missile batteries were being installed throughout Syria and that the Soviet Union had given the Syrian Air Force a number of MIG-23 planes, the most advanced in the Soviet jet fighter arsenal.

Nov. 19, 1974: A Defense Department spokesman reported that since January 1974, Syria had received 130 planes and helicopters including 45 Soviet MIG-23 jets and 30 Scud ground-to-ground missiles with a range of about 250 kilometers. The Syrians had also received 320 tanks, most of the T-62 variety and 115 ground-to-ground Frog missiles.

Soviet shipments to Syria since the beginning of the October war include:

SCUD missile launchers: 9-12 (none before the war)
Fighter aircraft: 120 (including about 60 MIG-23)
Helicopters: 15
Transport aircraft: 4
Surface-to-air missile batteries: 15-20
Medium tanks: 1,200
Torpedo boats: 4

Since 1974, Syria has also received Armored Personnel Carriers and artillery and electronic equipment. A new arms deal was concluded between the Soviet Union and Syria in October, 1975; the quantities involved are not known.

Major aircraft sales from the Western countries and the Soviet Union include: 130 MIG-21 fighter bombers and 45 MIG-23s.

Many of the sales have been financed by Saudi Arabia, Kuwait and the United Arab Emirates who have pledged to transfer weapons to the confrontation states in the event of another war with Israel. Press reports have alleged that Saudi pilots were flying their American-made F-5 fighters in Syria in conjunction with the Syrian Air Force. (Syria is a member of the League of Arab States; among its subsidiary bodies are: The Arab Defense Council, set up in 1950 and The Unified Arab Command, organized in 1964.)

THE SYRIAN ARMY: FIGHTING STRENGTH

Population: 7,370,000.
Military service: 30 months.
Total armed forces: 177,500.
Estimated GNP 1974: $2.9 bn.
Defence expenditure 1975: £Syr 2,500 m ($668 m).
   $1 = £Syr 3.74 (1975), £Syr 3.52 (1974).

Army: 150,000.
2 armoured divisions.
3 mechanized infantry divisions.
2 armoured brigades.
1 mechanized brigade.
3 infantry brigades.
8 commando battalions.
3 parachute battalions.
2 artillery brigades.
24 SAM batteries with SA-2 and SA-3.
14 SAM batteries with SA-6.
100 T-34, 1,300 T-54/-55, 700 T-62 med, 70 PT-76 lt tks; 1,100 BTR-50/-60, BTR-152 APC; 700 122mm, 130mm, 152mm and 180mm guns/how; 75 SU-100 SP guns; 140mm and 240mm RL; *FROG-7* and *Scud* SSM; 120mm and 60mm mor; *Snapper, Sagger, Swatter* ATGW; 23mm, 37mm, 57mm, 85mm, and 100mm AA guns; SA-2, SA-3, SA-6, SA-7, SA-9 SAM.

Reserves: 100,000.

Air Defence Command (under Army Command, with Army and Air Force manpower).
SAM batteries, AA arty, and interceptor ac and radar.

Navy: 2,500.
3 *Komar-* and 3 *Osa*-class FPB with *Styx* SSM.
1 T-43-class minesweeper.
11 torpedo boats (ex-Soviet P-4).
1 coastal patrol vessel.

Reserves: 2,500.

Air Force: 25,000; about 400 combat ac.
1 sqn with Il-28 lt bombers.
4 FGA sqns with 50 MIG-17.
3 FGA sqns with 45 Su-7.
2 FGA sqns with 45 MIG-23.
About 250 MIG-21 interceptors (more on order).
6 Il-14 and 3 An-12 transports.
Hel incl. 4 Mi-2, 8 Mi-4, 39 Mi-8, and 9 Ka-25.

Para-Military Forces: 9,500; 8,000 Gendarmerie; 1,500 Desert Guard (Frontier Force).

Source: *The Annual Military Balance, 1975-76,* p. 38, International Institute for Strategic Studies, London,1975. Reprinted by permission.

VI

Syria and Israel

1948-1967: The Period Between the Wars

Like the rest of the Arab world, Syria has never accepted the existence of Israel and has consistently labored to destroy it. The Syrian nationalists strenuously opposed the Zionist endeavor in Palestine. They saw the Balfour Declaration as a betrayal of their goal, which was that the Arab Middle East must remain under Arab hegemony. Syrians generally regarded the area of Palestine as "Southern Syria" and often referred to it in this way. Before the rise of Palestinian Arab nationalism (which in fact was inspired by the rise of Palestinian Jewish nationalism, i.e., Zionism) the Arabs of Palestine often spoke of themselves as Southern Syrians. In the amorphous entity that was the Middle East before the creation of separate nations, "Syria" embraced, in the Arab consciousness, many peoples, lands and regions.

In reaction to the U.N. resolution of 1947 to partition Palestine into two states, one Arab, one Jewish, Syria joined the other Arab states in condemning the U.N. resolution and in preparations to nullify it by military force. Armed Arab assaults on Jews in the mixed towns and along the highways immediately escalated. These were followed by more organized and concerted attacks by the Arab states and the Arab Higher Committee to prevent the Jewish state from being established. At the Arab Prime Minister's conference in Cairo on December 16, 1947, the Syrian Government was entrusted with the training and organization of Arab forces for intervention in Palestine. This took the shape of an "Arab Liberation Army," trained and equipped in Syria. As their numbers increased, the Arab forces penetrated into Palestine via Jordan and carried out systematic attacks against isolated settlements and cities with mixed populations. They cut off several Jewish settlements in the north and inflicted casualties on Jewish convoys in the south. The Jewish forces (Haganah) repulsed an Arab Liberation Army attack on the settlement of Mishmar Ha'emek and captured several Arab villages in Galilee.

The State of Israel was proclaimed on May 14, 1948. During that night the army of the newly created state of Syria was one of the seven Arab armies that invaded the new state of Israel. Syrian troops succeeded in occupying the eastern shore of Lake Kinneret and the area's evacuated settlements but were repulsed when, in a major operation, the Jewish forces occupied the whole of Upper Galilee. Syrian forces, however, managed to hold a narrow strip on the eastern shore of Lake Kinneret and a small area adjacent to the northeast corner of the Syrian-Israel border, two areas that were situated in territory that had been allotted to the Jewish state under the partition plan. When hostilities ceased, Syria was at first reluctant to enter into Armistice negotiations and proclaimed her policy of abstaining from any step which might imply acquiescence to the existence of the State of Israel. Syria used the first ceasefire of 1948 to establish its hold on the Golan and to fortify and consolidate its positions. In 1949, in accordance with the terms of the Armistice Agreement, Syria agreed to withdraw its forces on condition that these areas be demilitarized.

Syria, however, almost immediately violated the status of the demilitarized zone by taking al-Hamma by force of arms in 1951. It placed artillery batteries on advantageous positions overlooking the Huleh Valley and northern Galilee and frequently shelled Israeli farms and fishermen on Lake Kinneret. Between 1948 and June 1967, the area of the Israel-Syria Armistice demarcation line was consequently the scene of constant and serious fighting and shooting incidents.

The main problem concerned the legality of civilian activities in the demilitarized zone established by the Israel-Syria Armistice Agreement of 1949. The zone had been created primarily to meet Israel's demand for the withdrawal of Syrian troops from those parts of Israeli territory which they had occupied during the hostilities of 1948-1949. To achieve this withdrawal the Israel-Syrian Armistice Conference had decided that areas occupied by Syrian forces and some adjacent areas should constitute the demilitarized zone.

Between 1951-1953, Israel had two development projects—the draining of Lake Huleh and the diversion of part of the Jordan waters, which entailed work in the demilitarized zone. Syria challenged Israel's right to proceed with the projects in the zone, claiming that the zone was not under Israeli sovereignty. Syria also contended that Israel would acquire topographical military advantages with the completion of these projects and thus violate one of the provisions of the Armistice Agreement, since the demilitarized zone had been established to separate the armed forces of both parties. For its part, Israel maintained that the demilitarized zone was under Israel sovereignty and that the Armistice Agreement did not contain any injunction against the execution of civilian development works in the zone. Israel also argued that the provision for the separation of the armed forces of both sides did not entail the prohibition of non-military activities.

Other disputes concerning the demilitarized zone arose over the cultivation of land by the Israeli and Syrian residents in the zone. Both Israel and Syria supported the claims of their respective farmers to extend their cultivation, and many fields became the subjects of contention. These disputes gave rise to numerous shooting incidents which caused a steady deterioration of the security of the whole border area.

A fundamental conflict between Israel and Syria related to Syria's position on matters affecting the zone. In Israel's view, the Armistice Agreement did not confer any rights to Syria to determine policies relating to the demilitarized zone while Syria claimed that each party had an equal right to determine policies there. As a result of the controversy, the Mixed Armistice Commission was prevented from holding both ordinary and emergency meetings.

Israel and Syria also held opposing views with regard to civilian activities carried out in Israeli territory outside the zone. Syria challenged Israel's right to pursue the Huleh Drainage and Bnot Yaakov (diversion of part of Jordan's waters) projects outside as well as inside the zone. Syria's position was that the topographical changes so effected by Israel would create a military advantage for Israel, in contravention of the Armistice Agreement. Israel's position was that the question of military advantage was irrelevant, since the truce following the cessation of hostilities had been replaced by an Armistice.

Syria also opposed a third Israeli development project executed outside the demilitarized zone—the Lake Kinneret-Negev Project (Israel's national water carrier plan)—on the ground that it violated international law and was prejudicial to the security and interests of the Arab states. Israel contended that the project was fully consistent with international law and that its purpose and effects were confined exclusively to Israel's internal economic development.

Syria took particular exception to the patrolling by Israel police boats near the northeastern shore of Lake Kinneret. Syria considered these boats as naval craft, whose presence in an area defined in the Armistice Agreement as defensive was prohibited. Israel argued that the boats performed ordinary police functions and that their presence in the defensive area did not constitute a violation of the armistice terms.

Another cause of tension in the area of Lake Kinneret was a long-standing dispute over the right of Syrians to fish in the lake. Israel had objected to Syrians fishing in her waters without holding fishing permits issued by the competent Israel authorities. Syria asserted that fishing permits to Syrian fishermen should be issued by the Chairman of the Mixed Armistice Commission.

The situation gave rise to constant tension and bloody clashes, culminating in the war of June 1967. The following are among the incidents that occurred:

> On April 4, 1951, seven Israeli policemen were killed by soldiers of a Syrian outpost overlooking the road to al-Hamma and by armed Syrians shooting from the village. According to the Report received by the Mixed Armistice Commission, the policemen were killed in cold blood while on a routine patrol.

> Abba Eban, Israel's Minister for Foreign Affairs, reported to the U.N. Security Council that as a result of acts organized and executed by Arab governments, 137 Israel citizens were killed in 1951; 147 in 1952; 162 in 1953; 180 in 1954; and 258 in 1955.

> Incidents in the Lake Kinneret area reached a new peak in March 1962 when, according to a complaint from the Israel delegation to the Mixed Armistice Commission, the Syrian positions at al-Kursi opened heavy machine-gun, bazooka and recoilless gun fire on an Israel police boat. A Syrian complaint relating to the same incident stated that an Israel armored fighter had come within 40 meters of the eastern shore of the lake and had opened automatic fire on the Syrian position. Syrian witnesses testified that the Israel patrol boat had opened

machine-gun fire on farmers working near the village of al-Kursi. U.N. Secretary-General, Dag Hammarskjold, pointed out that the statement of the Syrian witnesses did not explain the damage done to the Israel police boat. Following several similar incidents (on March 8, 15 and 16) Israel took recourse to retaliatory action. The U.N. Security Council determined that the Israel attack (of March 16-17, 1962) constituted a flagrant violation of the Security Council resolution of January 19, 1956 calling upon the two Governments to refrain from the threat and the use of force.

There were 17 incidents of Syrian firing on Israeli fishing boats in the period from December 1962 to August 1963.

Relations between Syria and Israel became particularly strained after the abduction, on July 17, 1963 of three Belgian citizens—two brothers and their mother—and three Israelis—a man and two girls, who were rowing a boat on Lake Kinneret. A sudden wind had driven the boat toward the northeastern shore. Syrian soldiers held them up at gun point and forced them to cross into Syria, where they were imprisoned. The three Belgians were speedily released. The three Israelis were only released after strenuous diplomatic efforts, made with the active participation of U.N. Secretary-General U Thant and an exchange of prisoners was effected. On December 21, 1963, 11 Israelis were exchanged for 17 Syrians, seven of the Israelis emerged from the Syrian prisons as serious mental cases. Israel protested against their cruel treatment by Syria to the U.N. Secretary-General and to the International Red Cross Committee.

Syria claimed that since it was in de facto possession of the ten meter strip Israel was precluded from executing its Lake Kinneret-Negev Project. Israel saw this as a challenge to its use of the water for economic purposes.

A serious incident occurred on November 13, 1964 in the vicinity of Tel Dan. It arose out of a dispute over the question whether a patrol track built by Israel along the armistice demarcation line in that area encroached on Syrian territory. On November 1, 1964 Israeli workers began reconstructing a portion of the track west of Tel Dan. Israeli surveyors laid a white tape on the ground which was in no circumstances to be crossed, in order to avoid encroachment upon Syrian territory. On November 3, an exchange of fire took place after the firing by a Syrian soldier of what was described by Syrian witnesses as a "warning shot" in the direction of two Israeli bulldozers and a grader. According to the Syrian complaint about the incident, the construction work was being carried out in Syrian territory. The ensuing investigation, conducted by the Armistice Agreement Commission, did not definitely establish whether encroachments had taken place. Both Israel and Syria brought reinforcements to the area. On November 13, an Israeli patrol was fired upon from Syrian positions, immediately followed by machine-gun fire. The fire was returned. The intensity of the shooting increased, Syrian artillery and anti-tank guns then began firing from various other positions. Israeli aircraft attacked Tall 'Azazyat. During the subsequent investigation, the U.N. observers found evidence of severe Syrian shelling of three Israeli settlements. The UNTSO team which undertook the investigation of the Syrian complaint was informed by the Syrian authorities that it would not be permitted to visit most of the places detailed in the complaint as having been bombed by the Israeli planes. At Quneitra they were not permitted to inspect the casualties resulting from the shooting, but were informed that seven Syrians had been killed and 26 injured, most of them civilians. The U.N. Security Council failed to adopt a resolution on the incident.

On July 14, the permanent representative of Israel at the U.N., Mr. Michael Comay, informed the Security Council of a "sudden recrudescence of sabotage and road mining attacks on Israel border areas, carried out from Syria." He drew attention to four incidents which occurred on July 13 and 14 between Lake Kinneret and Metulla, resulting in the killing of soldiers and farmers. These Syrian activities had been accompanied by bellicose pronouncements by Syrian leaders inciting their people to a "popular liberation war" against Israel. Mr. Comay asserted that al-fatah operations had been the principal source of border tension and that al-fatah infiltrators had carried out 53 raids in Israel since January 1965, and that Israel's information indicated that Syria was the source, training ground, and the principal supplier and the main political patron of the organization. Syria had openly identified herself with al-fatah and claimed credit for its activities, Mr. Comay said. The "war communiques" of the "general command" of al-fatah were regularly published by the government-controlled Syrian press and broadcast by Radio Damascus. The organ of al-'Asifa (the military arm of al-fatah) had been officially published in Damascus since May 1965 and Syria had insistently demanded that the Arab leaders accept its proposals for an immediate military confrontation with Israel. The Syrian representative, Mr. Toma, reiterated that Syria was not responsible for the rise of Palestinian militant organizations and added: "Nor can Syria conceive its duty as being guardian or protector over what Israelis consider to be their frontiers." (U.N. S/PV 1288, 25 July 1966.) The majority in the Security Council, while deploring Israel's attack, held that the blame could not be put exclusively on one side. It failed to agree on a single stand with regard to the complaints placed before it.

On August 15, 1966 Syria mounted an air attack against two Israel police boats on Lake Kinneret. Following an investigation by the U.N. observers, the Chairman of the Mixed Armistice Commission drew the attention of the senior Syrian delegate to the fact that the Syrian air attack across the armistice demarcation line was a very serious violation of the Armistice Agreement.

On October 12, 1966 Israel requested an urgent meeting of the Security Council to discuss the "acts of aggression committed by armed groups operating from Syrian territory against the citizens and territory of Israel" and the "open Syrian incitement to war against Israel," in violation of the U.N. Charter and the Israel-Syrian Armistice Agreement. Israel's Minister for Foreign Affairs, Abba Eban, drew attention on October 11, to a statement made by Syria's Chief of Staff with reference to the operation of the Palestinian units: "These activities which are now being carried out are legal activities and it is not our duty to stop them but to encourage and strengthen them . . ." The representative of Syria, Mr. Toma, reiterated Syria's position that Syria was not responsible for the activities of al-'Asifa. Most members of the Security Council found Israel's grievances justified. The representative of the Soviet Union called Israel's allegations "built on sand" since the main premise had not been proved—that the guerrillas had acted from Syrian territory.

The following are some of the statements made by Syria during this period:

> To the question why we fight the Palestine Liberation Organization and support the al-'Asifa organization, the answer is this: We will not hesitate to praise the Palestine Liberation Organization if that organization will demonstrate that it is fulfilling its mission . . . every drop of blood that is spilled on the soil of Palestine brings us more honor than all the utterances outside those borders.
>
> Radio Damascus, October 4, 1965

> The correct principle is to be found in the (Ba'th) party's pronouncements: this is the principle of the war of liberation that is not based on the classic methods. The traditional war that is based on superiority in the quantity of arms will lead us nowhere. Therefore we have no choice but to launch a war of liberation . . .
>
> Major-General as-Swaydani, Syrian Chief of Staff, May 22, 1966

> We have adopted the popular liberation war as the basis of our action for Palestine out of the belief that the Palestine question is one of life and death to the Arab masses . . . Revolutionary Syria will continue its revolutionary policy until Palestine is liberated . . .
>
> President al-Atasi, August 20, 1966

> We have made all preparations for a full-scale popular war and shall take the battle from the frontier to the heart of the usurped land.
>
> Major-General as-Swaydani, August 23, 1966

After 1964, Syria formulated—and began to implement—a plan to divert the headwaters of the Jordan River, which channels a large part of Israel's water supply into Lake Kinneret. By 1967 Syria had transformed the entire Golan Heights and the border between Syria and Israel into a massively fortified area. It had the benefit of Soviet arms, which had been pouring into Egypt and Syria at an increasingly accelerated rate. Israel, in turn, fortified its positions, but on June 5 1967, had concentrated only a maximum of one infantry brigade and one armored brigade against the Heights.

The war of June 1967 was triggered by the actions of President Nasser, but Syria quickly joined the Arab expeditionary forces sent into Jordan and placed under Egyptian command.

On June 5, immediately after Israel's offensive on the Egyptian front, Syrian artillery bombarded Israeli villages in Galilee and Syrian forces attempted to capture Kibbutz Dan. Israel responded with a full-scale attack on the Golan. The Golan Heights[1] fell to Israel within two days, and Israeli forces began advancing on the main road to Damascus.

---

1. This area, of 444 square miles, is a mountainous region bordering on the Upper Jordan Rift Valley and Lake Kinneret in the west, the Yarmuk River in the south and the Hermon mountain range in the north.

After the war, it became evident to military observers that, in the course of nineteen years of tension and hostile relations with Israel, Syria had converted the Golan Heights into one huge, fortified camp. These fortifications were described by some military authorities as stronger than the Maginot Line (of World War II). There were three parallel lines of defense, comprising dozens of fortified points with overlapping fields of fire. One such point, for example, was a promontory two miles south of Baniyas and two miles east of Kibbutz Dan, which looked out across the Huleh Valley and the hills of Galilee. The positions in this fortified point were almost entirely underground and connected by a series of interlocking trenches some eight feet deep and three feet wide, some of which were finished with smooth stone and mortar walls, and all of which were perfectly camouflaged. The principal gun positions in the point were set in a concrete bunker with walls one yard thick. The city of Quneitra, near the Israel border and the hub of the Syrian heights and the gateway to Damascus, was found to be a labyrinth of well dug and camouflaged fortifications.[2]

2. Radio Damascus announced the fall of Quneitra on June 10, six hours before any Israeli troops reached it. The troops in Quneitra, convinced that they would not be reinforced from the rear, abandoned their positions and fled. Nadav Safran, in his book *From War to War* (Pegasus, 1969), suggests that the reason for the Syrian announcement may have been the fact that Quneitra had been so heavily bombarded by the Israelis that its ruins were no longer worth defending and that the Syrian forces could be better deployed in defense of Damascus.

The Factors Behind the 1967 Crisis

By JACOB ASCHER

Syria, as the cradle of Arab nationalism, has always regarded itself as being in the vanguard of the Arab states' struggle against Zionism. The territory of Palestine was once considered to be part of that country and it is perhaps for this reason that the Syrians have regarded the establishment of the State of Israel as constituting a great wrong done to the Arabs.

Since the war of 1948, Syria has been the most extremist of the Arab countries in its expressions of hostility toward Israel. This was due in part to a long chain of tensions along the Syrian-Israeli border which created problems that proved adamant to a solution and to the Syrian's denial of Israel's right to exist, which is embedded in the ideologies of all the various political trends in that country.

The Syrian army was the only Arab army to emerge with a feeling of victory from the war of 1948. It had not suffered a decisive defeat by Israel and it had even succeeded in holding on to some of its conquests within the area that had been allotted to the Jewish State in the 1947 partition plan. Armistice negotiations were protracted and difficult. The armistice agreement finally signed in July 1949 did not serve to solve the day-to-day problems along the Israeli-Syrian border and, in addition, Syria maintained that a status of truce existed only until the renewal of hostilities while Israel insisted that the armistice agreement constituted a state of true armistice which must eventually lead to a final peace settlement.

Syria's feeling of confidence was also based on its topographical situation. Its territory lay on an average of some 1,509 feet above Israeli territory for almost the entire length of the 47 miles of the two countries' common border. The Israeli side was populated by civilian settlements. The Syrians maintained fortified positions, with a small and scattered civilian population. They could therefore disrupt normal Israeli civilian life at will by use of artillery fire and without the necessity of concentrating large forces. Effective Israeli retaliation implied the use of the Israeli air-force and an escalation of hostilities. The Syrians became adept at this form of brinkmanship in the course of time: they would call a halt to the series of incidents whenever it appeared that the Israelis might be on the verge of launching a massive retaliation.

Article V of the armistice agreement, which dealt with the demilitarized zones (DMZ) (i.e., zones evacuated by the Syrian Army under the armistice agreement) was interpreted differently by Syria and Israel. The Israelis believed themselves to have sovereignty over these areas—except for restrictions

Mr. Ascher is a graduate of the Department of Middle Eastern Studies at Tel Aviv University, Israel.

on the type and amount of weapons and number of troops introduced into these areas. The Syrians felt they were entitled to participate in the administration of the DMZs and to intervene on behalf of its Arab inhabitants. They were totally opposed to any Israeli development projects in the zones and Israel had initiated its plans to drain the Huleh swamp and to construct the Bnot Yaakov irrigation project, which would have to be carried out, in part, in the DMZ.

Further causes of tension arose over lands cultivated in the DMZ. This was accompanied by Syrian attempts at infiltration and disruption of the work of Israeli farmers. The attempts by both sides to establish *faits accomplis* by cultivating lands in the DMZs led to constant incidents and culminated, in January 1960, in the penetration by Syrian forces into the southern DMZ. Israel retaliated on February 1, 1960 by an attack on Syrian positions at Tawafiq, which was a center of harassment of Israeli farmers in the area.

A major dispute arose over the diversion of the waters of the Jordan River and the attempts made by the Arab states in the region to divert its sources, which are found in Syria, Lebanon and Israel while a major tributary flows into it from Jordan. The river flows in Israel and Jordan and its waters are indispensable to the two countries. The U.S. sponsored a plan for the integrated exploitation of the water which would benefit all the riparian countries. Eric Johnston, the author of the plan and special representative of President Eisenhower made prolonged efforts from 1953 to 1955 to get the parties concerned to agree to this plan "on the technical level", including an allocation of percentages of available water. Although Johnston's final proposals were similar to those previously advanced by the Arab states, they refused, in the end, to participate in any regional project which would include Israel, since this could be construed as a recognition of the Jewish state. Syria took the leading role in this rejection, although implementation of the plan would have benefited Syria and Jordan as well as Israel.

In the circumstance, Israel initiated a plan of its own in 1959 and began to construct its National Water Carrier, to lead water from the Sea of Galilee to the Negev desert in the south of that country. Syria declared that the realization of the Israeli project would constitute a serious danger to Arab interests. The Jordan, Syria announced, was an international river and Israel could not be regarded as a party to affairs concerning this river.

Israel's National Water Carrier project became operational at the end of 1963. The Arab states, at the First Arab Summit Conference in January 1964, passed a resolution to divert the sources of the river in Syria and Lebanon. Israel regarded this as a hostile measure, since it would mean that the availability of the Jordan water, which was Israel's main source of irrigation, would be placed in jeopardy.

Lebanon was dissuaded, through various political measures, from implementing its project to divert the water when these plans were already at an advanced stage. The Syrian project was halted by Israeli artillery shelling.

When Syria moved its canal deeper into its territory, Israel bombarded it from the air. These activities led to the Third Arab Summit Conference, held in September 1965 at Casablanca, which reached the decision to postpone the Syrian and Lebanese projects.

Another issue was the problem of sovereignty over the north-eastern shore of the Sea of Galilee where the Syrians, who had occupied a narrow strip of land belonging to Israel, interfered with Israeli fishing and patrolling of the area. This led to innumerable incidents, culminating in the large-scale clashes of December 1955, March 1962 and August 1966. Several minor clashes also occurred over the border demarcation lines and, at the beginning of 1965, a new cause of friction occurred with the beginning of infiltration and sabotage operations inside Israel by Palestinian commandoes actively supported by Syria. These activities eventually led to the May-June 1967 crisis between the two countries.

On February 23, 1966, members of the left wing of the Ba'th party carried out a coup against the regime in Syria. Most of the new rulers were young army officers and many of them belonged to the minority groups, such as the 'Alawites and the Druze. Born in the late 1920s and early 1930s, the war of 1948 was for them one of their formative experiences and, as members of minority groups, their nationalism expressed itself in extremist and radical terms. The new regime soon found itself at loggerheads with the many internal factions in Syria and thus jeopardized its very existence. An especially grave crisis, which arose in early April, 1967 was only resolved with the heightening of the war psychosis in May of that year.

Two tendencies became conspicuous in Syrian foreign policy. One was its accelerated rapprochement with the Soviet Union. The USSR declared that it would not tolerate any act of aggression against Syria and that it could not remain indifferent to events in an area so close to its own southern border. The Soviet intervention prevented any political pressure from being put on Syria by the U.N. and encouraged the Syrians in their military preparations. The other tendency in Syrian foreign policy was its rapprochement with Egypt and the formation of the group of "progressive" Arab states headed by Egypt and Syria (as opposed to the "reactionary" Arab states headed by Jordan and Saudi Arabia). Egypt and Syria signed a mutual defense pact on November 4, 1966. It was regarded by Syria as a guarantee of Egypt's immediate military reaction in the event of an Israeli attack on Syria.

Syria's relations with Jordan, a member of the "reactionary" camp, were hostile. It encouraged fedayeen activity from Jordanian territory against Israel in order to set off Israeli retaliatory measures against Jordan and thus to help undermine the royalist regime and perhaps bring about its downfall. Israeli policy was to retaliate against the state from which the fedayeen had infiltrated but it became clear to the Israeli military that the source of the infiltration was not Jordan but Syria.

Syria responded to these Israeli charges by declaring the fedayeen activities legal and by denying any responsibility for them. As expressed by the Syrian Ambassador to the U.N. in a Security Council debate: "Syria cannot see it as its role to defend what Israel considers to be its borders."

The regime in Damascus placed its struggle against Israel on an ideological basis. In April 1966, it adopted the doctrine of a "popular war of liberation" as its official guideline. The enemy was defined as "an unholy alliance between imperialism, Arab reaction and Israel"—and the latter country was termed a danger to the Arab world and especially to the revolutionary regime in Damascus. The spearhead of the popular liberation war was the Palestinians, with the fedayeen as their vanguard. Hafez al-Assad, Syria's Minister of Defense at the time, proposed an aggressive strategy to be undertaken by the Syrian army in cooperation with fedayeen activity—a strategy which was conspicuously implemented in the year preceding the 1967 war. During this period the situation along the Syrian-Israeli border deteriorated significantly. Major incidents occurred on July 14, 1966, August 15, 1966 and April 7, 1967. The August clash presented two new features. The Syrians, for the first time, declared that the incident had been initiated by them and Israeli planes not only crossed the Syrian border but also pursued Syrian planes deep into Syrian territory. In the April 7, 1967 incident, initiated by the Syrians, Israeli planes penetrated to the suburbs of Damascus in their pursuit of Syrian planes and shot down 6 Syrian MIG-21s.

Following this clash, the Soviet Union spread rumors to the effect that Israel was concentrating troops along the Syrian-Israeli border. This triggered an Egyptian involvement on May 15, 1967, which led to the outbreak of war on June 5, 1967.

The Period 1967-1973

Syria accepted the U.N. cease-fire call of June 8, 1967, although it was not put into effect until June 10-11. After heated debate in the Security Council, it also agreed to the reestablishment of UNTSO. The war of 1967 was followed by U.N. Security Council Resolution 242 of November 22, 1967, which called for a final settlement of the conflict, an Israeli withdrawal from occupied territories, mutual recognition, and Israel's right to free passage through the Gulf of Aqaba and the Suez Canal. Syria did not accept the resolution and continued its adamant opposition to it throughout the period. It gave its negative reaction to the five-point general plan for peace advanced by President Lyndon B. Johnson on June 19, 1967 and also refused to accept the reactivation of the negotiations as provided for in Resolution 242 through the offices of U.N. representative Dr. Gunnar Jarring. It also refused to consider the Rogers peace proposals of June 25, 1970.

President Assad declared that Syria would reject Resolution 242 and all other proposals for securing an Arab-Israeli settlement through the U.N. or great power guarantees, which were all only "another form of occupation." The government continued to obstruct the work of UNRWA, as it had done in the past, despite the fact that a burden of new refugees had been added to those already in Syria since 1948, on the ground that any attempt to resettle or rehabilitate the refugees would prejudice their right to repatriation and would be an acknowledgement of Israel's existence.

To Syria, its border with Israel, from which it encouraged terrorist infiltration, continued to be "the armistice demarcation line." It consistently maintained a state of war with Israel and its belligerent statements only escalated with the passing years.

The following are among them:

> The hatred which we indoctrinate into the minds of our children from their birth is sacred.
>
> > From a letter by the Syrian Minister of Education to M. René Maheu, Director-General of UNESCO, reprinted in "A-Thaura," Ba'th Party organ, Damascus, May 3, 1968.

> The Regional Command of the Ba'th Party, in its official statement on November 16, 1970, castigated "surrender solution plans, especially the Rogers plan" in reference to the Arab-Israeli conflict.

> We must alert Arab minds to Israel's boundless ambitions—namely, the establishment of a Greater Israel from the Euphrates to the Nile within the framework of studied, scientifically-programmed, long-range planning . . . Israel's non-occupation of Lebanese territory does not mean it does not want this territory.
>
> > President Assad, in an interview with the Lebanese paper "Al-Bayrak," according to Radio Damascus, December 5, 1972.

> . . . The Zionist presence threatens all the Arab countries and the national existence of the Arab nation. Therefore, all the Arabs must make available all their resources and seek a formula for Arab action enabling our people to ward off the danger surrounding them and to liberate their land.
>
> > Syrian Deputy Premier and Foreign Minister, Abd al-Halim Khaddam, Radio Damascus, January 2, 1973.

Between 1972-October 1973, Syria received arms and equipment from the Soviet Union at an unprecedented rate. The weapons were deployed in a solid triple belt along the entire perimeter of the June 1967 cease-fire lines extending almost to the suburbs of Damascus. Syria had in addition acquired modern and highly mobile anti-aircraft and anti-tank missiles, and also offensive weapons such as the Frog missile and the T-62 tank, many of which had never before been sent outside the Soviet bloc. On the eve of the Syrian-Egyptian October 1973 attack on Israel, Syria had massed 1,400 tanks against a combined Israeli force of 180 and Syrian artillery outnumbered Israeli artillery by ten to one, but the Syrian offensive was repulsed by Israel within days.[3]

Before the cease-fire of October 22, 1973 was implemented, Israeli forces had occupied an area of 600 square kilometers extending from the foothills of Mount Hermon to the Damascus-Quneitra axis, thus bringing the outskirts of Damascus within Israeli artillery range.

The Mount Hermon range, which is the common border of Israel, Syria and Lebanon affords, on its peaks, a virtually unlimited view from the Mediterranean to Damascus and from the Huleh Valley to Lake Kinneret. Israel gained complete control of the range and established a presence on the mountain's peak, literally "blinding" Syria's view of Israel or Israeli-occupied territory.

Syria-Israel Relations After October, 1973

Security Council Resolution 338 of October 22, 1973 reads:

> The Security Council,
> 1) Calls on all parties to the present fighting to cease all firing and terminate all military activity immediately, no later than 12 hours after the moment of the adoption of this decision, in the positions they now occupy;
> 2) Calls on the parties concerned to start immediately after the cease-fire the implementation of Security Council Resolution 242 in all of its parts;
> 3) Decides that immediately and concurrently with the cease-fire, negotiations start between the parties concerned under appropriate auspices aimed at establishing a just and durable peace in the Middle East.

The resolution had been drafted by the U.S. and the Soviet Union and it was therefore expected that Syria, as a Soviet client, would agree to its terms. Dr. Kissinger, the U.S. Secretary of State, who had been the chief instrument in arranging the cease-fires, began a new round of shuttle diplomacy in an effort to

---

3. According to Riad Ashkar, in "The Syrian and Egyptian Campaigns," *Journal of Palestine Studies*, Vol. III, No. 2, Winter 1974, a cause of the collapse of the northern sector of the Syrian front could be blamed on a Syrian colonel, commanding a brigade, who attempted to advance more rapidly than other Syrian units and was cut off from the main body of the army. The brigade was compelled to withdraw when the Israeli counter-offensive began thus creating confusion in the Syrian lines. Other accounts accuse the Syrian commander of panicking and ordering a disorganized withdrawal without the consent of the Syrian high command.

get the parties to the conflict to Geneva, where they could hammer out their differences and achieve a final peace settlement. Israel and Egypt sent their delegations to Geneva. Although it soon became clear that the talks would not involve negotiations on peace but only on disengagement, Syria refused to send its delegation to Geneva. It declared that it would not consider the talks as direct negotiations with Israel and that it rejected the idea that the Arab states would have to recognize Israel or sign a peace agreement with it in accordance with Resolution 242—which it did not accept in the first place.

Despite its heavy losses (7,000 killed and 21,000 wounded of 120,000 troops, according to the annual report of the International Institute for Strategic Studies, May 9, 1974) and the general disruption the war had brought, Syria declared itself ready to renew the war and indirectly castigated Egypt for entering into the disengagement talks.

The Syrian attitude was greatly influenced by several factors. Syria had lost additional territory in the war—Israel had captured a further 845 square kilometers on the Golan Heights—and with this loss of territory had come a new loss of prestige, particularly since Egypt, for its part, had succeeded in regaining a part of Sinai. Syria was also afraid that Egypt, despite President Sadat's assurances that any settlement achieved with Israel had to be tied to a similar settlement with Syria, would go back on its word and would work for a separate disengagement agreement. In order to hamper this agreement Syria now used its only real weapon—the fact that it held some 65 Israeli POWs—as its leverage. It refused to release the names of the POWs and refused to consider an exchange of prisoners "unless this was part of a unilateral Israeli withdrawal from all occupied Arab territories."

The POW issue was especially painful for Israel, both in the light of Syria's known treatment of the Israelis it had captured in previous years and following Israeli discoveries of murdered and mutilated soldiers in newly occupied territory. In the latter case, the atrocities revealed were so abhorrent in nature that the original Israeli complaint to the International Committee of the Red Cross had not been submitted to the UN. Syria's intransigence on the POW issue drew international protests. As Simone de Beauvoir wrote (*Le Monde,* Dec. 17, 1973): "If Syria goes on trampling on the rules respected by all nations to limit horrors of warfare, then their action can be summed up in only one word: barbarism."

Under Soviet pressure (there had been an exchange of high level visits in January, 1974) Syria indicated that it might consider going to Geneva if the Soviet Union would give its support for disengagement talks that would not commit Syria to negotiate with or recognize Israel. Syria now also insisted on receiving a territorial gain—the return of the city of Quneitra.

Israel, through Dr. Kissinger, declared its willingness to permit the return of an estimated 20,000 civilians and farmers who had been driven out of their homes in the fighting to the newly captured Syrian salient and also agreed to hand over two Syrian installations on Mount Hermon to the UN buffer forces, in the framework of a separation of forces agreement which permitted the return of the Israeli POWs. While emissaries from Saudi Arabia and Egypt travelled to Syria to persuade President Assad to enter into a disengagement agreement and to moderate his attitude on the POWs, Syria announced a "War of Attrition" against Israel, "to force Israel to keep its reserves on active duty and to paralyze its economy."

It was widely reported that the war of attrition was fully supported by the Soviet Union. Soviet Foreign Minister Andrei Gromyko visited Syria in order to accelerate Soviet plans to re-equip the Syrian army and to ease the financial terms for purchases of arms. In a joint communique on March 7, 1974, Gromyko and Assad declared that any separation of forces agreement "must be the first step of a total Israeli withdrawal from all occupied Arab territories, in accordance with a determined timetable." The Soviet Union, it added, affirmed Syria's "legitimate right to employ all effective means to liberate the occupied territories."

The fighting on the Golan which began on March 11, 1974 continued in the midst of Dr. Kissinger's negotiations. In April, Syria demanded the return of three hilltops, strategic positions formerly manned by Syria to control much of the northern Golan plain, in addition to the first Israeli concessions. As Syria was preparing to enter into a disengagement agreement, sentiments inside Syria were whipped up against Israel. The Syrian Ba'th party paper, *Al Thawra* declared in an editorial (May 11, 1974):

> If we assume the efforts for a peaceful settlement will succeed and will lead to a phased Israeli withdrawal from Arab lands, we must start planning for the next stage from now. We must start planning for the next stage so as to be able to continue to push the enemy out of our occupied lands.

Thousands of May Day demonstrators paraded down the streets of Damascus carrying signs which read: "We Declare that Palestine is an Inseparable Part of Syria," and "Kissinger: The Jewish Conspirator."

The separation of forces agreement between Israel and Syria was announced on May 29, 1974 and signed at a ceremony in Geneva on May 31.

In 1974, Syria turned to another front of attack: it became the champion of the Palestinians, wresting this role away from Egypt. President Assad publicly introduced this policy in a speech on March 8, 1974, on the occasion of the eleventh anniversary of the Ba'th party's rise to power in Syria. The true interpretation of Resolution 242, he said, called for:

> . . . return of all territories captured in June 1967 and the return of the rights of the Palestinians. Syria will accept nothing less . . . The Israeli authorities would do well to be reminded that we view Palestine not only as an inseparable part of the Arab nation, but also as part of Southern Syria.

On May 23, 1974 Israeli forces wiped out an eight-man squad of the *Popular Democratic Front for the Liberation of Palestine* which had been on its way from Syria to what was described by one of the survivors as a raid to capture Israeli children in Israeli settlements in the style of the *Ma'alot* terrorist attack on a school (May 15, 1974). The Syrian government issued a communique on the mission, which read:

> There are some points which Syria refuses to discuss such as the question of the fedayeen. He who wishes to discuss this subject must solve the Palestinian issue and debate the problem with the Palestinian leadership. Any other attempt is a waste of time.

There were numerous other incidents of infiltration from Syria and statements regarding its training and encouragement of terrorist activities, including the PLO raid on the Hotel Savoy in Tel Aviv on March 6, 1975. When asked, in a TV interview in the U.S. on March 7 if his country supported the attack, Syria's ambassador to Washington, Sabah Kabani said:

> Of course, not only Syria—all the Arabs.

The raid was carried out while Dr. Kissinger was attempting to effect a second stage Israeli-Egyptian agreement, as an apparent warning to Egypt that it would face isolation if it acted unilaterally.

One of the expectations arising from the disengagement agreement had been that Syria would reconstruct the town of Quneitra, and thus help to bring about a normalization of the area which Israel had returned as part of the agreement. This expectation has not, so far, been fulfilled. Syria has argued that the Israelis had deliberately destroyed the town before leaving and has declared that this destruction was so thorough that the town would be uninhabitable for many years to come. Syria also broke the disengagement agreement by paving a road on the Hermon ridge leading to its peak. In place of returning 100,000 civilians to the abandoned settlements around Quneitra, it has expanded its military presence in this area. It has installed 160 mm. mortars in excess of the limited number of such weapons permitted in the thinned-out forces zone and in addition maintains a number of tanks in standing positions and above the ceiling authorized by the agreement.

The Syrian-Israeli disengagement agreement stipulated that the UN force's mandate is for six months, and that it is renewable subject to the parties' consent. Syria has to date, consented to renew this mandate preceded each time by a war of nerves and open threats to renew the fighting. Its attitude to Israel remains as was expressed most succinctly by Syrian Minister for Culture and National Guidance, Dr. Fawzi al-Kiali, in a lecture in Beirut (published by *Al Nahar*, December 15-17. 1974):

The Arabs constitute a great power in the world—the sixth greatest power according to the world press and the British Institute for Strategic Studies. The factors creating this power of the Arabs are—territory, a large population, geographic locale, natural resources, cultural level and the tremendous income from oil . . . Zionism sprang from the ghetto and the rise of world imperialism was the factor that turned Zionism from a Fascist dream to a Fascist fact . . . Aside from the logic of force . . . Israel is nothing but a geopolitical fantasy, a weak disjointed patch-quilt package of disintegrating religious falsehoods, Fascist paranoid illusions and sick historical aberrations . . . We must understand that our struggle with the enemy is long and hard. It is an all-out struggle . . . first and foremost, the modern and effective preparation of Arab military power is the only way to assure our prospects for advancement and development and against the treachery and foolishness of Israel . . .

Lt. Colonel Al-Hizham al-Ayoubi, a former officer in the Syrian army and later military chief of the *Popular Front for the Liberation of Palestine,* reiterated the Syrian view in an interview (October, 1974) with the Palestinian journal, *Shoun Falastiniya:*

The strategic outlet is continuation of the state of no-peace, rejection of any freezing of the Palestinian problem or disengagement from it in any way; maintaining the psychological pressure and measured military tension; cultivating the latent state of hostility and the capacity to effect an armed confrontation, large or small, when made possible by the appropriate local or international circumstances . . . Until fulfillment of the Arab demands that Israel withdraw to the borders of 1948, the Arab states will wage conventional yet short wars, each of them in reality an attack in the continuing procession of guerrilla warfare. The connection will thus have been created between conventional action within the overall framework of a long-term war of attrition as a manifestation of guerrilla warfare. Afterwards, when the political settlement is achieved, it will be the turn of the fedayeen to act . . .

The theme has been constantly repeated. On November 25, 1975, following the murder of three unarmed Israeli students by terrorists infiltrating from Syria, Twefik Hassan, commentator of the government-controlled Radio Damascus stated:

Syria is working to mobilize all the Arab resources, including the sabotage organizations, both militarily and on the oil front, to open up an all-out Palestinian war against Israel whose purpose is to free Palestine from the racist Zionist entity, and this by relying on the internationally supported Arab strategic depth . . . Syria's firm stand is the rock on which Israel shall be destroyed together with all imperialist, racist and Zionist plots.

Military Significance of the Golan Plateau

By IRVING HEYMONT

Terrain studies show that the most significant military feature of the Golan Plateau is the very restricted access to the area from Israel. More specifically, the western edge of the plateau is a steep escarpment that rises abruptly to heights of 400 to 1700 feet above the floor of the Huleh valley—one of the richest agricultural areas in Israel. This escarpment is almost a vertical wall that extends from the northernmost point of Israel to a point just north of the Sea of Galilee. From this point the escarpment runs slightly east of the Sea of Galilee and drops somewhat in elevation. The southern boundary of the Golan Plateau is the gorge of the Yarmouk River which is also the boundary with Jordan. The pre-1967 Armistice line between Israel and Syria, for all practical purposes, was this escarpment and the western shore of the Sea of Galilee.

Peacetime access from Israel to the Golan Plateau across the escarpment is limited to the highway from Haifa to Damascus. This road cuts through the escarpment at about the midpoint and crosses the Jordan River at the Bnot Yaakov bridge not far from the Kibbutz Ayelet Hashahar. The other two roads from the west leading into the Golan Plateau, before 1967, were outside of Israel. One road was just north of Dan in the northeast corner of Israel and the other, in the south, was around the southern edge of the Sea of Galilee, through the gorge of the Yarmouk and then up on to the plateau. All three roads converged at the town of Quneitra which is located at the high point (elevation 3,950 ft.) on the ridge that runs southeast from the Mt. Hermon range (high point, 9,200 ft.) which dominates the Golan Plateau from the north.

The Golan Plateau, in the possession of a friendly neighbor, is of no importance to Israel. However, in the hands of a foe it is an extremely troublesome area. From the western edge of the Golan it is only about 60 miles, without major terrain obstacles, to the Haifa-Akko area—the industrial heartland of Israel. Further, the Golan escarpment dominates the fertile Huleh Valley enabling the Syrians, before the 1967 war, to bring the agricultural settlements under accurate artillery bombardment because these fires could be directed by observers on the ground. The problem was compounded by limitations on Israeli options to respond. Counterbattery fires were limited by the lack of effective observation from the Huleh Valley; air attacks were degraded by well dug-in Syrian positions with strong overhead cover, and a ground attack against the positions covering the escarpment would require major forces with attendant risks of heavy casualties and severe political repercussions. In the

Col. Heymont, Retired, U.S. Army, is associated with the General Research Corporation, Operations Analysis Division, McLean, Virginia.

1967 war, the Israelis took these risks and stormed the escarpment and breached the Syrian defenses but at a heavy cost in casualties. The Israeli losses were probably attenuated by the defeat of Egypt and Jordan just prior to the attack on Syria. The morale and determination of the Syrian forces had probably been severely undermined by the rout of the Egyptian and Jordanian armies. The news of this rout was undoubtedly known to Syrian soldiers who had transistor radios in addition to their weapons.

Given a continuing threat from Syria, the possession of some part of the Golan Plateau is a necessity for the security of Israel. This need is not solely to protect directly the Huleh Valley settlements from bombardment by ground weapons. The need is also to secure an area for ready deployment of Israeli ground forces to deter a ground attack on Israel in view of a possible quick Israeli reaction. The Golan Plateau and its continuation to the east contains no major terrain obstacles except for the escarpment leading to the plateau from the Huleh Valley. The settlements in the Huleh Valley can be brought under fire from long-range missiles such as the Soviet FROG and SCUD missiles that are readily available to the Syrians. The use of such missiles against targets in the Huleh can be expected to be deterred if the Israelis are in a position to threaten swift ground attacks against vital Syrian areas. This situation prevailed between the 1967 and 1973 wars and can be expected to continue unless the Syrians precipitate another full scale war as they did in October 1973. Further, the possession of some part of the Golan Plateau provides Israel with a buffer space that in the event of a surprise conflict reduces the possibilities of ground combat within Israel itself. This was the case in the 1973 war when the Israelis were able to reinforce their forces on the Golan with mobilized reserve ground units within 18 to 24 hours.

The depth of the area required on the Golan Plateau, to include the adjacent parts of the Mt. Hermon range, need be only enough to permit the deployment of ground combat forces and large enough to support some civilian and paramilitary settlements. If the area is too wide, the ability of Israel to react quickly on the ground is reduced unless large forces are maintained in the area at all times. The presence of civilian and paramilitary settlements in the area would enhance security by reducing the temptation for the Syrians to occupy the area by infiltration or a lunge forward with small forces. The southern part of the Golan Plateau is quite fertile and can sustain economically viable agricultural communities.

The 1967 Armistice line on the Golan Plateau runs slightly east of Quneitra. The resulting Israeli-held area meets the requirements outlined above. Any permanent extension of the Israeli-held area deeper into Syria to the east would add little to the security of Israel and might even detract by over extension of Israeli capabilities. However, the 1967 Armistice line is not the only one that would provide security for Israel, there are others that are also satisfactory, such as the one that resulted from the aftermath of the October 1973 war.

VII

Syria in the International Community

Syria at the United Nations

Syria became a charter member of the U.N. on April 12, 1945. By 1971 it had become a member of fourteen international organizations, most of them associated with the U.N.

The Syrian Arab Republic became eligible for a term as a member of the U.N. Security Council in 1969 and was elected to the Security Council on October 21, 1969.

The following are excerpts of the Syrian position, as expressed by the Syrian Representative in the U.N. Security Council in January, 1976:

> *Mr. ALLAF (Syrian Arab Republic):* In accordance with its resolution 381 (1975), adopted on 30 November 1975, this honourable Council is meeting today to debate the Middle East problem including the Palestinian question. In so doing, the Council is marking the beginning of a new and important phase on the way towards establishing a just and lasting peace in a region which has suffered from injustice and aggression for as many years as the United Nations has been in existence.
>
> That historic resolution, adopted by the Council on the initiative and urging of the Syrian Arab Republic on the occasion of the extension of the mandate of the United Nations Disengagement Observer Force in occupied Golan, reflects a positive and conscious exercise by the Security Council of its grave responsibilities under the Charter as the main organ for the maintenance of peace and security in the world. This is particularly true as the Council has, for the first time in its history, decided to discuss the Palestine question, the very core of the Middle East problem and its main cause, in a practical and substantive manner, rather than confining itself, as in the past, merely to discussing the repercussions of that tragedy and its side issues.

· · ·

> One of those parties directly concerned has chosen, however, not to show up; and one does not need to wonder very long to guess the reasons. It is true that a criminal would not feel very much at ease in the courtroom where his crimes were being considered and judged. Yet, we do not think that is the only reason why the Zionist aggressor has preferred to stay away. As a matter of fact, at the very moment when the important discussion on the question of Palestine and the Middle East started yesterday, the representative of the Zionist entity, instead of being here at this table at least to try to defend or justify the crimes and the wrongdoings of his racist régime, was right across the street, outside the United Nations, where he should really be permanently, attacking the United Nations and the Security Council, asserting that Syria and the PLO are preparing the stage

for a new round of fighting just because they have asked the Security Council to discuss the Middle East and the Palestinian question, and reaffirming the treatment that his racist régime usually reserves for all United Nations resolutions by declaring:

"Any Council resolution regarded as inimical to Israel's interests will join hundreds of other United Nations resolutions"—where?—"in the waste-paper basket."

*   *   *

The plain truth is that the Zionist régime is absent from this debate only because it has no real desire for peace. The Zionists are afraid of peace because peace can only be based on justice, and the racist Zionist régime could not survive if justice were to prevail.

*   *   *

The tragedy that has befallen the Palestinian people is the source of the present conflict in the Middle East. It was the cause of four bloody wars that flared up in the region during a period of less than 30 years. As a result of the colonialist-racist conspiracy, originally plotted at the first Zionist Congress in Basel in 1898 and further elaborated in the Balfour Declaration of 1917, so aptly described as "a promise by him who does not own to him who does not deserve" Arab Palestine was chosen to become the prey of covetous world Zionism, the most fanatic and discriminatory movement in modern history.

During the 30 years that followed the Balfour Declaration, forces of colonialism joined with those of world Zionism to carry out the conspiracy in successive stages and through deliberate and carefully studied steps.

In collusion with the British Mandatory authorities, the Zionists began flooding the Palestinian homeland, overtly and covertly, with hundreds of thousands of invading immigrants. They expropriated lands from their rightful Arab owners through deception and temptation, or by terrorism and threats, and the uprisings and revolts of the heroic Palestinian people between the two World Wars could not stop the waves of the Zionist colonialist and racist invasion, which was clearly aimed at Judaizing Palestine and usurping it from its lawful owners.

In continuation of the conspiracy, the British Government brought the Palestine question before the newly born United Nations in 1947.

*   *   *

During the 20 years that followed [the Partition Resolution] the Zionist-racist cancer kept spreading and expanding into other parts of the land of Palestine and the Arab nation . . .

. . . The October War of Liberation of 1973 provided unmistakable conclusive evidence that the Arab people would not allow one inch of their territories to remain under occupation, and would not remain silent over the slightest violation of any of the inalienable national rights of the Palestinian people.

*   *   *

However, the Zionist-racist entity soon forgot the lessons of the October War of Liberation. In fact, shortly after that war, Israel resumed its arrogance and intransigence, and persisted in its expansionist and racist policy and in its rejection of peace . . .

. . .

The Arab States remained, as they still are, in a state of war with Israel throughout the 20 years from 1948 to 1967, though not a single inch of their land was under occupation during that period. The main cause of the conflict has always been— and still is—the Zionist aggression against the land of Palestine and its people. Inasmuch as the Zionist aggression against the Arab people did not start on 5 June 1967, the solution of the Middle East conflict cannot be based on resolutions or solutions that take into account only what has happened since that date. This explains the inadequacy of Security Council resolution 242 (1967) for securing the establishment of a just and lasting peace in the Middle East, even if the Israeli aggressors were to implement the said resolution, although this has by no means happened. Resolution 242 (1967) was adopted under the impact of the treacherous Israeli aggression of June 1967 and was intended to deal with the immediate consequences of that aggression. It cannot replace, nor can it claim to replace, previous United Nations resolutions relating to the Palestine question or the Middle East problem. It cannot supersede those resolutions. If resolution 242 (1967) could cancel previous United Nations resolutions, such as, for instance, resolution 181 (II) of 29 November 1947 providing for the establishment in Palestine of an Arab State and a similar State for the Zionists, then it would mean that the resolution under which, according to the United Nations, the State of Israel was established, had become null and void.

. . .

Those who are stipulating the termination of the state of belligerency in the area prior to the complete withdrawal from all the occupied Arab territories or prior to the ending of the violation of the inalienable national rights of the Palestinian people are in fact putting the cart before the horse; they are beginning to read the book from its last page. Even those who, with the best intentions, are advocating an end to the state of belligerency and some other characteristic conditions of peace at the same time and on the same level as they advocate withdrawal from the occupied Arab territories and recognition of the inalienable rights of the Palestinian people—even they are confusing the causes and the consequences, are mixing up the pre-conditions for peace with peace itself.

United Nations Security Council, S/PV. 1871, 13 January, 1976

Mr. ALLAF, (Syrian Arab Republic): . . . It is really regrettable to see one of the two greatest super-Powers dedicating its influence and its policy to the service of the aggressor. People have long ago begun to wonder who is really conducting the foreign policy of the United States of America. Is it President Ford or Mr. Rabin? Who decides about the action of the United States delegation? Is it Mr. Kissinger or Mr. Allon? This same question arises equally in relation to the question of who implements the policy of the United States in the United Nations. Is it Mr. Moynihan or Mr. Herzog? *The New York Times* of this morning gave a very timely answer to this last question. It said: "Mr. Rabin will be arriving in Washington at a time when Daniel Patrick Moynihan is serving as the Israeli voice in the United Nations Security Council."

Why is such a great Power as the United States of America behaving in this manner? The bitter fact is that the United States of America is only isolating itself. With a very small number of States it isolated itself in the past in the General Assembly and it is now doing the same thing in the Security Council. The tyranny of this minority will not prevent the process of a just peace. A just and lasting peace is going to be realized and established. Every inch of the Arab occupied territory will be liberated and the heroic Palestinian people, sooner or later, will enjoy every single one of its national inalienable rights. The only loser will be the United States of America itself, which has proved once more that it is supporting the aggressor and that it lacks any quality of fairness, any quality which would make it a neutral and acceptable mediator in the Middle East crisis.

United Nations Security Council, S/PV. 1879, 26 January, 1976

Syria's Relations With the U.S.

By ELIZABETH L. CONROY

United States recognition of Syria on September 7, 1944, and the establishment of diplomatic relations, inaugurated the beginning of an often difficult relationship. From then until 1950 relations were relatively cordial, but were marred by U.S. support for the establishment of the Jewish state in Palestine and by U.S. recognition of Israel in 1948.

When, in March 1949, a military junta under the leadership of Col. Husni Zaim took control of the Syrian government, the United States accorded recognition to the new regime, which it viewed as reformist and not revolutionary. This perception was reinforced by Zaim's assurances that Syria would honor its international commitments and that elections would be held as soon as possible. When Zaim was assassinated (August 14, 1949) the new military regime was recognized by the United States on September 20, 1949. When still another coup d'etat took place in 1951, no formal recognition was accorded the regime of Col. Adib Shishakli; instead an American diplomat called at the Foreign Ministry and this ceremonial visit was viewed as an indication of recognition by the United States.

Continued support for Israel and United States' efforts to get recognition for Israel by the Arab states produced noticeable strains in the relationship. In early May 1951 the United States extended an offer of technical aid to Syria under the Point IV program, but on June 8, 1951 the offer was rejected on the grounds that Israel was to receive a large share of the total funds allotted. In October 1953, President Eisenhower sent Eric Johnston as a special representative to the Middle East to discuss development of the Jordan River Valley by the riparian states. The United States expected that the regional states would implement a unified development plan for irrigation projects, water storage and hydroelectric plants and that this would increase the stability of the area, promote economic progress and provide land for use by the Palestinian refugees. Syria was willing to support the plan in principle, but the inclusion of Israel, which implied sovereignty and therefore recognition of its statehood, was a stumbling block to Syrian acceptance of the plan. The other Arab states were also unwilling to support the project, and it eventually lapsed.

Another factor that led to increased tension between the two countries was American pressure for a Middle East collective security system. In February 1955 Syria repudiated these efforts when it rejected participation in the Baghdad Pact. The preoccupation on the part of the United States with the possibility of increased Soviet influence in the Middle East had been the primary reason for its support of the Pact, and it was also the rationale behind the Eisenhower Doctrine which was formulated in January 1957. The Syrian government rejected the idea of a vacuum in the area or of a Soviet threat. Rather, Syria was more concerned with imperialism and with Zionism, which it perceived as far greater threats to Syrian national interests. As a result of these American activities in the Middle East, Syria felt that the United States was trying to take the place of the French or the British and that the Eisenhower Doctrine was a means by which the United States could interfere in Arab affairs. For its part, the United States viewed Syrian overtures to the Soviet Union during 1957 as imperiling the stability of the entire region. By August 1957 U.S.-Syrian relations had become so strained that three American diplomats were expelled from Syria because the Syrians charged them with being implicated in a plot to overthrow President Shukri al-Quwwatli's regime. The United States retaliated by expelling the Syrian envoy and the Second Secretary of the Syrian embassy.

The formation by Syria and Egypt of the United Arab Republic (UAR) in 1958 brought some amelioration of the tense relations. The newly formed government was recognized on February 25, 1958 and the United States embassy in Damascus became a consulate, with diplomatic relations being handled by Cairo. During this period, Nasser was regarded as a salutary check upon Syria's dangerous tendencies toward closer relations with the Soviet Union. Although actions by Syrians in the Lebanese civil war of 1958 again increased tensions, diplomatic relations were not severed nor was there a rupture when the United States troops landed in Lebanon to help prevent Syrian subversion following the Iraqi *coup d'etat* of July 15th. The Syrians were given a strong warning by the United States ambassador to the United Nations that an attack on U.S. soldiers would lead to grave consequences and no untoward incidents occurred.

When Syria seceded from the UAR in 1961, the United States granted it recognition and an embassy was reopened in Damascus. There was a period of political turmoil in Syria in the early 1960s and Syrian governments changed rapidly. The United States granted formal recognition only to the regime established in November 1961 and then again to the Ba'thist government in 1963. In the years that followed, no additional recognition was considered necessary by either the United States or Syria, because each new government was considered to be a continuation of the same regime. The radical nature of the Ba'thists and Syria's close connections with the Soviet Union prevented positive interaction with the United States during the 1960s. These years were marked by another expulsion of U.S. diplomats and continued recriminations by Syria about U.S. imperialism and support for Israel.

The outbreak of the June 1967 War resulted in Syria's breaking diplomatic relations with the United States on June 6, on the grounds that the United States aided Israel in the conflict. Syria regularly attacked the United States and its support of Israel during the period from 1967 through 1972. The Syrians accused the United States of trying to overthrow progressive, or radical, regimes and of trying to frustrate resistance movements, as well as attempts to create a diplomatic atmosphere that would assure Israel's success in holding its 1967 gains. At the announcement of the U.S. decision to supply Israel with Phantom jets in December 1968 and again on their delivery in 1969, Syria denounced the United States' actions. The U.S. initiative of June 1970 was vehemently rejected by Syria, and Egypt and Jordan were castigated for accepting the Rogers Plan. Despite the verbal attacks which continued during 1970 and 1971, the United States indicated, on several occasions, that it considered the Assad government a moderate one, and expressed cautious hopes that a normalization might be possible.

After the October 1973 war the situation changed dramatically. At the end of October, U.S. Secretaty of State Kissinger had a private meeting with the Syrian Vice Minister of Foreign Affairs, Zakariya Isma'il, at the United Nations. Kissinger attempted to persuade the Syrians to participate in talks on a disengagement of forces on the Golan Heights. This initial contact was not productive, but in December Kissinger was able to make some progress toward re-establishing diplomatic contacts. Early in 1974 two American diplomats were sent to Damascus to open an American interests section at the Italian embassy. When Kissinger was negotiating the Egyptian disengagement of forces in the Sinai, he also went to Damascus. He returned to Israel with a list of Israeli prisoners held by the Syrians and then took Israeli proposals on the Golan Heights disengagement to the Syrian government on the 1st of March and in April the Syrians sent representatives to Washington to discuss the proposals.

During May, Kissinger began the Syrian phase of "shuttle-diplomacy" and travelled between Damascus and Jerusalem almost constantly.[1] The first visits were exploratory in nature and Kissinger did little more than take Israeli views to Syria and bring Syrian views back to Jerusalem but the talks soon progressed to discussions of specific issues. After each meeting in Damascus, Kissinger referred to the cordial character of the meetings, and reported that progress was being made. On May 22nd Kissinger hosted a luncheon in Damascus at which Syrian Foreign Minister Abd al-Halim Khaddam declared that he felt that a new relationship with the United States was emerging and that American policy was beginning to change. He gave credit for this to Kissinger. The negotiations on the disengagement of Syrian troops had also resulted in greatly improved relations between Syria and the United States and in a greater understanding of their mutual problems.

On the 12th of June the Department of State requested that the Congress permit a portion of its contingency fund for the Middle East be used for aid to Syria, if concrete requests were forthcoming. The matter of aid for Syria had

1. Kissinger was in Damascus on May 3/4, 8, 12, 14, 16/17, 18, 20, 21, 22, 23, 26/27, 28, and 29.

been raised for the first time in April, when Kissinger had indicated that this fund was available for use if Syria and Israel would agree to disengagement talks similar to those held by the Egyptians. Over the years from 1946 to 1974 Syria had received no military assistance from the United States and no Export-Import Bank loans. The total economic assistance for Syria from the U.S. in this period amounted to $61 million and this was in emergency relief under the Food for Peace program. Between 1949 and 1952 the United States supplied Syria with only $400,000 in aid, between 1953 and 1961, with $36.4 million, and between 1962 and 1974 only $19.7 million.[2] Following the disengagement agreement, U.S. assistance figures showed a substantial increase. In November 1974 a U.S.-Syrian economic agreement was signed for $22 million and in June 1975 the United States agreed to lend Syria $58 million for development projects. The American aid to Syria was given primarily as a gesture of good-will and to indicate the U.S. willingness to cooperate with the Syrian government.

On the 15th of June 1974, President Nixon became the first American President to visit Damascus. When Nixon left Damascus the restoration of diplomatic relations between Syria and the United States was announced. Nixon invited President Assad to visit the United States, but on August 22 to 25 the Foreign Minister came instead. In October Kissinger returned to Damascus to review U.S.-Syrian relations, which were perceived as improving steadily. The Secretary of State hoped that a new negotiating process could be arranged, but he did not expect large-scale results from his visit.

By November, however, Syrian disenchantment with Kissinger's peace efforts were becoming apparent, and in December the Syrians rejected President Ford's proposals for a step-by-step Middle East settlement, charging that the U.S. and Israel wanted to nullify the Security Council's resolutions calling for Israeli withdrawal from the occupied territories. This did not disrupt contacts between the two governments and Kissinger returned to Syria in February and March 1975. However, the Syrian stance hardened against his incremental approach to negotiations and Syria began to insist upon unified discussions on all aspects of the Arab-Israeli dispute. When Khaddam returned to Washington in June to talk to Ford and Kissinger, his visit provided no new impetus for further negotiations. In an effort to placate Assad and to restore cordiality to the relationship Kissinger went to Damascus in August 1975 with an offer to act as negotiator for a second stage agreement on the Golan Heights. Syria would not agree to begin negotiations again but it did not reject the possibility of a demilitarization there. President Assad's conditions for further

---

2. Department of State, Agency for International Development, *U.S. Overseas Loans and Grants and Assistance from International Organizations July 1, 1945-June 30, 1974*, p. 25. In 1962-65, 1966, and 1967, Syria received less than $50,000 in military aid and the entire total of military aid from 1946-1974 was $100,000.

negotiations were that a timetable be established for withdrawal of troops on the Golan Heights, that the rights of the Palestinians be recognized and that the Palestine Liberation Organization participate in the peace talks. The U.S. veto early in 1976 of the Arab-backed Middle East Resolution in the United Nations displeased Syria and further strained the relationship.

Even though relations between Syria and the United States experienced a setback from the cordial shuttle-diplomacy period, they did not return to the level that existed before the October 1973 war. While remaining critical of the U.S.-Israeli relationship, Syria found it possible, due mainly to Kissinger's efforts, to deal with the United States rather than totally rejecting diplomatic contact.

In the present U.S. perception, Syria appears to have become an important factor in the U.S. effort to bring stability to the Middle East.

VIII

Syrian Views

On Israel

We are ready to live in peace with Israel in exchange for total withdrawal from all Arab lands but we will not recognize her. Never.

> President Assad in an interview with the New York Times,
> Sept. 28, 1975.

Syria's ideological and fundamental position finds expression in the effort to mobilize Arab forces so as to bring their military resources and their oil, together with the Palestinian Revolution, to bear on the execution of a campaign of liberation on all the fronts, aiming at the implementation of the UN resolutions. This will be a Palestinian campaign, aided by the Arab 'hinterland' with all its potential, as well as the international 'hinterland'—for legitimization . . .
Syria did not agree with Egypt on the termination of the state of war (with Israel) or on the commitment for the non-use of force and the removal of the economic boycott of Israel.
The Arab people everywhere is fully aware of Syria's firm stand. Syria is the rock on which Israel's expansionist ambitions will be smashed.

> Radio Damascus, Nov. 25, 1975.

Palestine is Southern Syria.

> President Assad, on the eleventh anniversary
> of the revolution, March 8, 1975.

It was Syria from which Palestine was severed and from the territory of which Israel was created.

> Syrian U.N. delegate at the Security Council
> debate of June 9, 1967: U.N. Document S/PV 1352

It might be useful to remind those in power in Israel that Palestine is not only part of the Arab homeland but is a principal part of Southern Syria . . . Palestine will remain part of the liberated Arab homeland and part of our country—Arab Syria.

> President Assad, Radio Damascus, March 8, 1975.

Our region will not witness stability unless our cause has been solved and the Arab people of Palestine got his just rights completely.

> President Assad, as reported in Flash of Damascus,
> November, 1975.

The Corrective Movement has restored to Syria its leading role by launching a wide campaign to achieve Arab solidarity and mobilize Arab potentials to serve the Arab struggle for liberation.

> Flash of Damascus, November, 1975.

On Jordan

Syria and Jordan are one nation, one homeland, one army.

President Assad on his visit to Jordan, June, 1975.

On Lebanon

Syria and Lebanon are a single country. We are more than brothers . . . Syria's economic prosperity . . . guarantees the future of the Lebanese people.

President Assad in an interview with Al-Anwār.
August 10, 1972.

Lebanon will not escape from the destined unity of Syria and Lebanon.

Syrian Minister of Information, Ahmed Iskander,
Jan. 1975.

The defense of Lebanon is an integral part of the defense program of Syria and the Palestinian revolution.

Zuheir Muhsin, Secretary-General of Sa'iqa

It is difficult to distinguish between the security of Lebanon, in the wider sense of the word, and the security of Syria.

President Assad, in an interview with al-Hawādith,
Middle East News Agency, June 25, 1975.

Relations between Syria and Lebanon are determined "by their community of destiny and fate."

Syrian Foreign Minister, 'Abd al-Halim Khaddām,
Syrian Arab News Agency, June 30, 1975.

Anyone who oppresses Lebanon, oppresses Syria.

Syrian radio commentator,
Radio Damascus, Nov. 8, 1975.

On Syria's Role in the Arab World

Circumstances make it imperative that Syria should assume the position of leadership in the Arab world.

Syrian Minister of Information Iskandar Ahmad

Syrian political circles speak of "Damascus becoming the new Cairo of the Middle East."

AP, reporting from Damascus, Nov. 21, 1975.

On the War of October, 1973

He butchered three of them with an ax and decapitated them. In other words, instead of using a gun to kill them he took a hatchet to chop their heads off. He struggled face to face with one of them, and throwing down his ax managed to break his neck and devour his flesh in front of his comrades.

This is a special case. Need I single it out to award him the Medal of the Republic? I will grant this medal to any soldier who succeeds in killing 28 Jews, and I will cover him with appreciation and honor for his bravery.

> General Mustafa T'las, Syrian Minister of
> Defense, eulogizing a hero of the October
> 1973 war before the Syrian National Assembly.

From the time it was launched, the Corrective Movement has stressed the supreme importance of mobilizing all Arab potentials to liberate the occupied Arab territories and restore the national rights of the Palestinian people. The October war of liberation represented an impressive manifestation of this trend.

> Flash of Damascus, November 1975.

Question:

In his recent speech President Sadat made slight of the counterattack which Syria was planning for . . . what is your answer to that?

Answer:

For President Sadat to say that is painful, and regrettable. As for the counterattack, it was clear, on the 15 of October and after, that the enemy had got involved in a pocket (strip of land) not more than ten kilometres in length and depth. Four enemy divisions were besieged by one of our infantry corps and two armoured corps, in addition to a reserve corps that arrived there on October 21, 1973, and in addition to two Jordanian armoured divisions. Orders were given by President Assad to cut the enemy forces, route and catch them as prisoners or destroy them. Preparations for the counterattack were almost ready when President Sadat's telegram was received, announcing his acceptance of a ceasefire. That was the most disastrous piece of news received throughout the whole war.

> General M. T'las, Syrian Minister of Defense in an
> interview with Flash of Damascus, November, 1975.

On Zionism

The purpose of Zionism and world imperialism is to take over Arab society in general, so that they can plunder its resources. The chief tools for the conduct of ideological terror are the traditional Arabic broadcasts of Radio London, the Voice of America and the stations of Tel Aviv, Bonn and Radio Free Europe. After them come the pro-imperialist stations like those of Holland, Belgium, Italy and others. These stations broadcast 92 hours a day in the Arabic language.
The question might be asked: is this because of their great love for the Arabic language?

Dr. Azat Ajan in an article in al-Ba'th,
Damascus, January 19, 1975.

Apparently no one listened to the content of the songs of Joan Baez and this is very unfortunate. For she is a Zionist, and devotes most of her songs to glorifying Israel . . . In one of her songs, she says: 'Here I'm standing in the station with a ticket in my hand to the Promised Land. I hope, I'm sure, I wait all night to leave for the Promised Land . . .'
In another song, Joan Baez says: 'Twelve gates to the city—Hallelujah. I look at the children. They wear clothes of red. There's no doubt, these are the children that Moses led through the desert.'
Every song has words of praise for the invasion and the conquest of the Arab lands. It should be made known that Joan is one of Zionism's biggest supporters.

The Syrian government newspaper, A-Thawra, in
a June 1975 article, attacking Ms. Baez for
her choice of American gospel songs during
her Baalbek (Lebanon) concert.

. . . Zionist racism is not a matter of political practice alone, for Zionist literature is rife with such phrases and terms as "Oriental barbarism" or "the super-nation," a term coined by Ahad Haam, a leading spiritual Zionist.

Flash of Damascus, November, 1975.

IX

Syria: A Political Directory

'Aflaq, Michel

Founder and ideologist of the Syrian Ba'th party. Born in Damascus in 1910 of Greek Orthodox Christian origin. 'Aflaq studied in Paris and was close to the Communist Party. He founded the ''Arab Renaissance Party'' *(al-Ba'th)* with Salah-ul-Din al-Bitar in 1940. This party united with the ''Arab Socialist Party'' of Akram Haurani in 1953, to become the ''Arab Socialist Renaissance Party.'' 'Aflaq stood unsuccessfully for parliament in 1947, but was appointed Minister of Education and then was defeated once more in the next elections. He remained Secretary General of the Ba'th party. He headed the ''civilian'' or more moderate faction when the Ba'th party came to power once more following the coup of March 1963. Both he and his faction were expelled from Syria in the coup of February 1966. 'Aflaq remained at the head of the ''National Command'' of the party, seated in Beirut and then Baghdad. 'Aflaq lived in Lebanon, emigrated to Brazil in 1967 and returned to Beirut and Baghdad in 1969. His book, ''In the Ways of the Ba'th'' (1959) is the standard textbook of Ba'th party doctrine.

Assad, Hafez Al-

Born in Lataqia, of 'Alawi origin. Has been a member of the ''national'' (i.e., all-Arab) Ba'th party and the Syrian High Command of the Ba'th since the 1960s. Was appointed commander of the Syrian Air Force in 1963. He belonged to the extreme left and the ''military wing'' of the Ba'th, led the military wing's coup on February 23, 1966 and became head of the temporary regime and served as Defense Minister. During this period he opposed total identification with the Soviet Union, called for a pragmatic approach to economic problems and for closer all-Arab cooperation and the resumption of the struggle against Israel. He gained control of the government in the spring of 1969 in a semi-coup and assumed full control in November 1970, as Prime Minister. He was elected President of Syria in 1971, as the sole candidate. Despite his ingrained mistrust of Egypt, born in the days of the U.A.R., Assad worked for a rapprochement and also brought Syria into a proposed, still projected ''Federation of Arab Republics.'' The Syrian-Egyptian cooperation of October 1973 ended soon after the war in mutual mistrust and vituperations.

Bitar, Salah-Ul-Din-Al

Born in 1912 in Damascus. Was a student at the universities of Damascus and Paris. Co-founder, with 'Aflaq, of the Ba'th and editor of its organ, *al-Ba'th*. As Syria's Foreign Minister, 1956-7, he worked for the union with Egypt. Was Minister of State for Arab Affairs in the first U.A.R. government and then Minister of National Guidance. He resigned in 1959 when Nasser began to curb the power of the Ba'th leaders. He headed five Ba'th governments after the break-up of the U.A.R., but was ousted in the coup of February 23, 1966. He was arrested but escaped to Lebanon and was expelled from the Syrian Ba'th party.

Eastern Command

This was created in 1968 as a joint command of Jordanian, Iraqi and Syrian forces with an Iraqi officer at its head. (Iraq sent troops to Syria and Jordan.) The Eastern Command was part of the Egyptian-headed Supreme Arab Unified Command set up in 1964 and which was never officially dissolved despite its failure to function in the Six Day War. The Eastern Command lost its effectiveness completely during the war between Jordan and the Palestinian organizations, who were supported by Syria and Iraq. Its value disappeared when Syrian forces invaded Jordan in September 1970. Although the Jordanian and Syrian armies reverted to their respective countries' commands, it was decided that the two armies should continue to aim at coordination and cooperation. The latest Syrian-Jordanian rapprochement, leading to the creation of a Supreme Coordinating Committee appears to be a step in that direction.

Feisal I, (b. Hussein), King

1885-1933: King of Iraq, 1921-1933. The third son of Sharif (later King) Hussein. Grew up in Constantinople and returned to Hejaz when the British appointed his father the Emir of Mecca in 1908. Feisal established ties with Arab nationalists in Damascus during World War I. He took command of the "Arab Revolt" in Hejaz in 1916 and entered Damascus as part of General Allenby's Allied Forces on October 1, 1918, becoming the King of Syria in the name of Arab nationalism. Ousted by the French on July 24, 1920, he presented his dynasty's claim to an independent Arab kingdom at the Paris Peace Conference and secured the throne of Iraq with the approval of Winston Churchill, T. E. Lawrence and the British "Arab Office" in Cairo.

Feisal, contacted by Chaim Weizmann as head of the Zionist Commission in Palestine, signed a conditional agreement with the Zionist leadership on future cooperation between the Zionist movement and the future Arab state on January 3, 1919. His statement on the compatability of Arab and Zionist national aspirations was published in *The Times* of London on December 12, 1918. The statement and the subsequent Feisal-Weizmann agreement are never mentioned by the Arabs, although Feisal is generally regarded as a leader of Arab nationalism.

Hashemites, Greater Syria and the Fertile Crescent

Toward the end of the Ottoman Empire, in the nineteenth century, the area of the Middle East extended in an unbroken line from Anatolia to Egypt. There were no national frontiers, no linguistic, natural or racial boundaries of importance, no passport controls or customs barriers. By 1922 this vast area had been carved up into eight administratively autonomous units by Britain and France. It became the main objective of Arab nationalism to free and reunify these territories.

The Sharif Hussein of Mecca, King of Hejaz (the Kingdom of Hejaz existed until 1925. The throne was lost to Ibn Saud [of what became Saudi Arabia] who captured Mecca and Hejaz) and who was the head of the House of Hashim, took the growing young movement of Arab nationalism under his auspices in 1916. From then on the fortunes of the movement could not easily be distinguished from those of the Hashemite family and in particular, from the career of Feisal, Hussein's third son. The Sharif envisioned an Arab empire with himself at its head, but when it became clear, after World War I, that Anglo-French interests and domination were to remain in the Middle East, Hussein and his sons agreed on a family program which, although never fully realized, explains much of later Hashemite behavior, and perhaps also modern Syrian and Iraqi thinking.

The family compact has been described as an understanding that Ali, Hussein's eldest son, would become King of the Hejaz upon his father's death. Abdallah, the second son, would become King of Iraq. Feisal, the third son, would become King of Syria.

Feisal succeeded in carrying out his part of the compact when he proclaimed himself King of Syria in 1918. His father, the Sharif Hussein became King of the Hejaz with the Emir Ali as his Heir Apparent. Feisal was however, ejected from his new kingdom by a French army in July 1920. Instead of going back to Hejaz, he went to the Peace Conference at Paris and, with British support, emerged as the candidate for the throne of Iraq, and was crowned King in Baghdad in 1921.

His brother, the Emir Abdallah was left without a kingdom. Abdallah recruited a private army and announced his intention of marching on Syria to expel the French. On his way he entered the newly British mandated territory east of the Jordan, set up a central administration in Amman and took over the whole area in March 1921. Accepting a fait accompli, the British announced that they were prepared to recognize him as ruler of this area.

The Hashemite failure to carry out their family plan gave rise to two powerful currents of thwarted ambition. Feisal and his heirs were determined to return to Damascus and liberate Syria and this idea became a main plank in the pan-Arab program. It provided a great part of the justification for the plan of Fertile

Crescent unity which was advanced by Nuri al-Sa'id of Iraq during World War II. Abdallah's ambitions did not come to rest in TransJordan. His plan for a "Greater Syria" was one of the motive forces of his political efforts.

In a proclamation to "the people of historical Syria" made on April 8, 1943, King Abdallah addressed the "people of Ash-Aham (Syria) . . . from the Gulf of Aqaba to the Mediterranean Sea and up to the Upper Euphrates." He described Syria as having been "dismembered." Syria was "pondering its re-unification, the mending of its rifts and the realization of its idea and forever proclaiming that it was—in its natural borders—one homeland linked by national, geographical and historical unity. (*Mudhakkirat al-Malik Abdallah Bin Al-Husayn* [King Abdallah's Memoirs], pp. 226-227.)

Pan-Arab aspirations at this time were to liberate Syria from the French, to eliminate the Jewish National Home in Palestine and to unite the Fertile Crescent under an independent Arab regime. Western hegemony over the Levant became, therefore, the primary target for pan-Arab attack. Even the Palestinian Arabs, in their struggle against the Zionist endeavor in Palestine, tended to talk of themselves as "Southern Syrians." It was seen by them as a way of joining the struggle against the British mandatory authority as well as against the Jewish community in Palestine.

Nuri al-Sa'id's Fertile Crescent scheme and the Emir Abdallah's "Greater Syria" received their first formal expression during World War II. In a "Note on the Arab cause with particular reference to Palestine and suggestions for a permanent settlement" presented to the British Minister of State for the Middle East, Richard Casey, Nuri al-Sa'id proposed a two-stage plan. Stage I was to be the union of Syria, Lebanon, Palestine and TransJordan into one state, with semi-autonomy under international guarantee for the Jewish minority in Palestine and safeguards for the Christians in Lebanon. Stage II was that "Greater Syria", when formed, should immediately join Iraq in an Arab League.

Abdallah was only really interested in the first stage of this scheme. His proposal was the immediate merger of TransJordan and Syria. It met with small encouragement from the British, but they agreed that the project could be studied pending a suitable occasion for its implementation.

At the opening of parliament on November 11, 1946, "Greater Syria" was formally proclaimed a principal of the newly independent TransJordan's foreign policy. King Abdallah, in his Speech from the Throne said: "We desire . . . immediate unity dictated by the longing of the country and its righteous sons . . . Our objective is stability in this western part of the Arab land overlooking the Mediterranean." (*Al-Kitab al-Urdunni Al-Abyad, p. 240*). The resolution of the TransJordanian government adopted July 1, 1947, and conveyed by King Abdallah to the British Government July 2, 1947, speaks of "the Arab countries including Syria, Lebanon, TransJordan and Palestine which all constitute historical Arab Syria." It refers to Jordan as "part of the entire country of Syria since the earliest historical times." The resolution also states that "the country of Syria, by virtue of its geographical position and its natural resources will not bear . . . to live (in anything) but one entity with its parts mutually supporting one another." (*Al-Kitab al-Urdumnni al-Abyad,* The Jordanian White Book. Amman, 1947, pp. 33-35). He wanted, Abdallah told the press, a state which included Syria, TransJordan, Palestine and Lebanon and saw only a single country bounded to the west by the sea, to the north by Turkey, to the east by Iraq and to the south by Hejaz. This country, he said, constituted Syria.

In August 1947, he called a meeting in Amman of "regional Syrian governments" to discuss his plans for union. These encountered extreme hostility in Egypt, Lebanon and Syria itself. President Quwwatli of Syria publicly denounced Greater Syria upon his re-election in 1947. The Syrian Chamber met in special session to protest unanimously against the project, which they declared, concealed personal ambitions, Zionist designs and threats to Syria's independence and sovereignty. Abdallah's sole supporters in Syria were the traditionally pro-Hashemite Jabal Druze on the TransJordan frontier.

Abdallah's advances to the Hashemites of Iraq had equally little success. He discussed the possibility of a union between the two countries with his nephew, the Regent of Iraq in 1945 and 1946 and made a number of proposals, such as that the two kingdoms should become one, but these were stillborn.

The interest of Iraq and TransJordan in Syria never developed into a political union of the Fertile Crescent. The division between the Hashemites and the nationalists and the emergence in 1945 of a rival pattern of inter-Arab relations in the Egyptian-dominated Arab League were among the reasons for this failure.

Abdallah's concern with Syria nevertheless continued until his assassination in 1951. Iraqi ambitions toward Syria remained a permanent feature of Syrian political life until Syria's union with Egypt in 1958.

King-Crane Commission .

This Commission, headed by Henry C. King and Charles R. Crane of the U.S. was sent to Palestine and Syria in 1919 to investigate the wishes of the population on the future of the two countries. The Commission reported to President Wilson that the Arabs were antagonistic to Zionism and to the imposition of a French mandate in Syria. Its majority opinion recommended that a "Greater Syria"—to include Lebanon and Palestine—be established and reported that the inhabitants of the areas (i.e., the Arabs) would prefer an American or a British mandate to a French mandate if one was to be established. A minority opinion dissented to the "Greater Syria" recommendation. Captain Yale reported that in his view "Palestine should be under the British who should be allowed to work out the Zionist question according to their lights and along reasonable lines." With guarantees for the Palestinian Holy Places, the Zionists "should be given their opportunity to work out a Jewish Common-wealth." He did not agree to a union of Syria and Lebanon—the Lebanese, he had found, did not want a union with Syria.

McMahon-Hussein Correspondence

An exchange of ten letters (from July 14, 1915-March 30, 1916) between Sharif Hussein of Mecca and Sir Henry McMahon, British High Commissioner in Egypt, discussing the terms for the Sharif's alliance with the British and his revolt against the Turks. Hussein demanded British recognition of the indepen-dence of the Arab countries and support for the reestablishment of an Arab caliphate. Britain accepted these principles but disagreed with Hussein's de-mand that the whole Arabian peninsula (except Aden) and the whole Fertile Crescent be included in this caliphate. McMahon's letter of October 24, 1915 stated: "The districts of Mersin and Alexandretta and portions of Syria lying to the west of the districts of Damascus, Homs, Hama and Aleppo, cannot be said to be purely Arab, and must . . . be excepted from the proposed delimitation." This later gave rise to a dispute between Britain and the Arabs, who maintained that Palestine was not part of the excluded area. Britain argued that she had never intended to include Palestine in the area of Arab independence. This was confirmed by McMahon in a letter to the Colonial Office dated March 12, 1922.

Palestine Liberation Army

Commander: Yasser Arafat
Chief of Staff: Brigadier General Misbah al-Budeiri
Estimated Fighting Strength: 3-5 Brigades; 5,000-17,000.

The PLA was created in 1964 as the military arm of the PLO and in order to organize the Palestinians' military potential within a regular military framework. The PLA's forces are stationed mainly in Syria and Egypt. Its headquarters are in Damascus. The PLA is under the jurisdiction of the Executive Committee of the PLO. Of its known forces, its *Hittin* and *Kadsiah* Brigades (consisting of 3 battalions each) are stationed in Syria. Its *Ein Jalout* Brigade (of 3 battalions) is stationed in Egypt. Its *Masab Ben Amir* battalion was stationed in Lebanon prior to the civil war and its *Zeid Iben Kharta* battalion is stationed in Jordan. Some two to three more battalions were sent to Lebanon from Syria during the civil war and have actively participated in the fighting.

All PLA battalions consist of infantry troops. Auxilliary weapons, mortar and light artillery rockets are also employed, including (in 1975) some light anti-aircraft missiles. There have been reports that the PLA also has Soviet-made T-34 tanks.

Yasser Arafat is responsible for the PLA's overall policies. Budeiri, who is a Syrian-trained Palestinian officer, supervises its day-to-day activities. The PLA has frequently been beset by conflicts between the military command and the PLO's political leadership.

The PLA's 5 brigades are reported to be equipped with 100 tanks and 2,000 armored cars. It has no air force, but 1,000 of its officers have been trained in Syria, Egypt and Iraq as pilots and aircraft maintenance specialists.

According to the *New York Times,* (January 22, 1976) the PLA's largest force is the *Yarmouk* Brigade, formed in 1970 after the civil war in Jordan, and consisting of some 1,500 Palestinians who had served with the Jordanian army. This brigade has been built up to a force of 5,000 trained in shock-troop tactics and is also stationed in Syria. It was transferred from the Jordanian to the Lebanese border and is reported to have played an active part in supporting the Palestinians in Lebanon.

In Syria, the PLA works closely with the Syrian army. In Egypt it operates in coordination with the Egyptian army.

The PLA fought as part of the Syrian and Egyptian armies during the war of October, 1973. Some PLA forces spearheaded the Syrian attack in the Golan Heights during the first days of the war.

Sa'iqa, Al ("Lightning")

Founded in 1968 in Syria by the ruling Ba'th party and the Syrian Army, this leftist Palestinian organization is under the direct command of the Syrian Army and its intelligence service. It includes Syrian soldiers and volunteers. Also called "The Vanguard of the People's War of Liberation" its headquarters are in Damascus, today headed by *Zuheir Muhsin*. Purges and factional rivalries in the organization reflect the factional rivalries inside the Syrian Ba'th Party itself.

Sunni(te) Muslims

The Islamic faith which swept across the Middle East in the seventh century and thereafter is the ruling faith of the Arab Middle East. It has shaped the social patterns and modes of thought and in many cases also the constitutions of several Arab states. The Sunnites and the Shi'ites are the two main divisions in Islam. The chief and major stream are the Sunnites who follow the *Sunna,* the traditional practice of the Prophet Muhammad as set forth in the *Hadith* (Traditions). The majority of Muslims in Syria are Sunnites.

Sykes-Picot Agreement

In 1916 Britain, France and Russia, the chief allies of World War I, exchanged secret notes about the partitioning of the Ottoman Empire. The agreement takes its name from the chief British and French negotiators, Sir Mark Sykes and Charles Francois George-Picot. In accordance with the Agreement, the non-Turkish provinces of the Ottoman Empire were to be divided between the three powers. The Arabian peninsula was to become independent. Palestine, west of the Jordan River (and excluding the Negev area) was to have an international regime while Britain was to be in direct control of Haifa and Acre and the region between them.

The French sphere of influence was to include the interior of Syria (Damascus, Homs, Hama, Aleppo and the Mosul District—Zone "A") and Cilicia and all of coastal Syria west of zone "A" (the "Blue" Zone).

The British sphere of influence was to include—Zone "B"—the Negev desert in Palestine, the area east of the Jordan River and central Mesopotamia reaching to Persia in the north and the Persian Gulf in the south. A "Red" Zone (the provinces of Basra and Baghdad) was to come under direct British control.

Zones "A" and "B" were planned as the areas of semi-independent Arab states or a confederation of Arab states to which France and Britain would supply advisers and where they would be accorded economic privileges.

Russia approved the Agreement in return for British and French recognition of its rights to annex certain areas in Anatolia. The Arabs and the Jews of Palestine criticized the Agreement as inconsistent with promises made to them both by Britain. The final redistribution of the Ottoman Empire changed certain of the Agreement's provisions. The Mandate system abolished formal, direct possession by Britain and France; Palestine became a British Mandate, Cilicia remained part of Turkey and France ceded her rights in the Mosul region to Britain. The Agreement was made public—and was repudiated—by the Bolsheviks in 1917.

X

Appendices

SYRIA UNDER OTTOMAN RULE

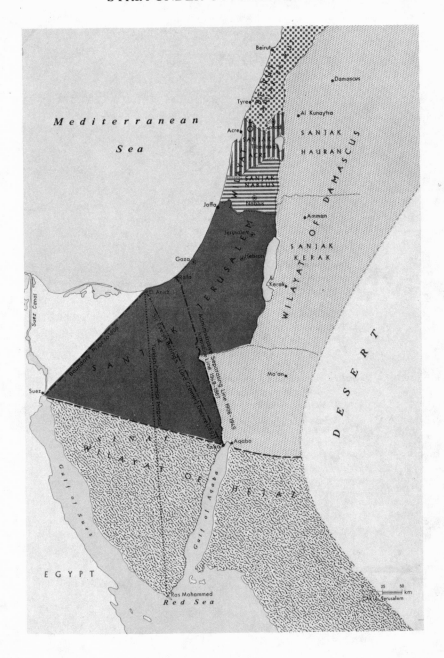

SYRIA-ISRAEL ARMISTICE LINES, 1949

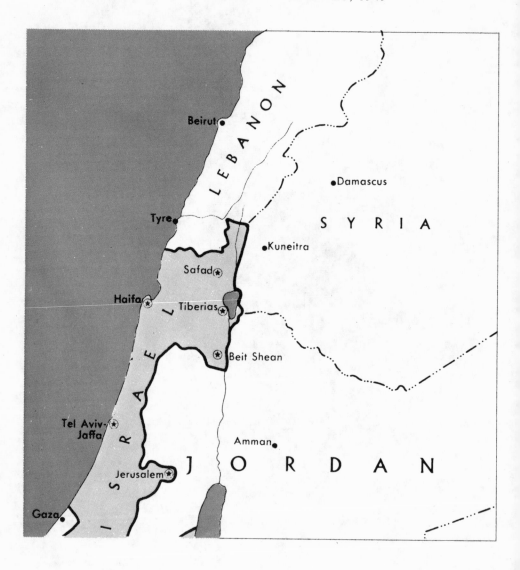

SYRIA-ISRAEL ARMISTICE LINES, 1967

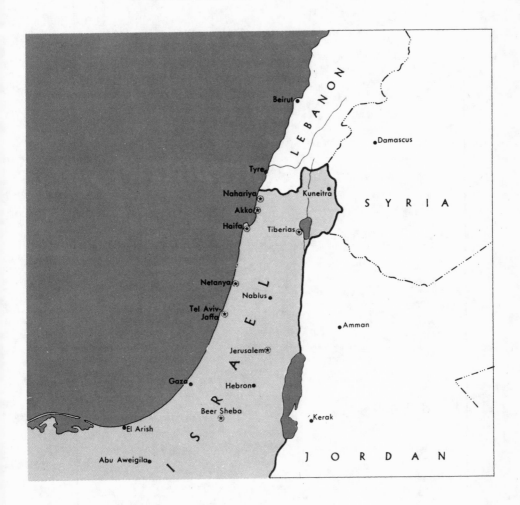

AREAS DESIGNATED IN AGREEMENT ON DISENGAGEMENT BETWEEN ISRAELI AND SYRIAN FORCES, 31 MAY, 1974

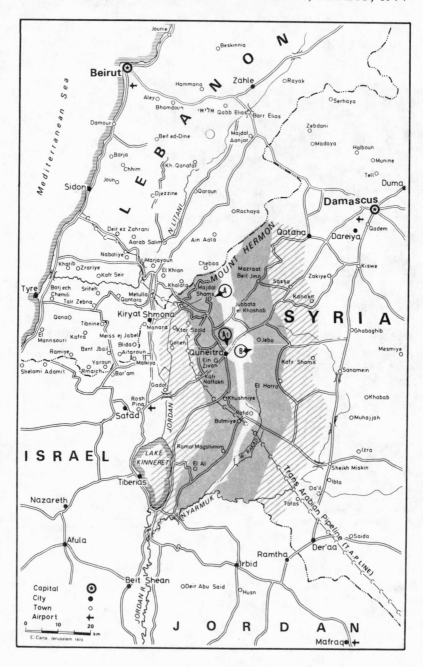

Constitution of the Syrian Arab Republic

PREAMBLE

When united, the Arab Nation played a great role in the development of human civilization; but when its national solidarity weakened, its civilization role receded and waves of colonial invasions were able to shatter its unity, occupy its lands and plunder its resources.

Faced with this challenge, the Arab Nation firmly rejected the imposed realities of dismemberment, exploitation, and regression, prompted thereto by the belief in its ability to overcome those realities and to reenter history and play, alongside other liberated nations, a special role in building up civilization and progress.

Close to the end of the first half of the present century, the struggle of the Arab people, in various countries was extended and intensified to achieve liberation from the direct colonialism of occupation.

The Arab masses, however, did not consider political independence a final objective and the end of all struggle and sacrifices. They regarded it rather as a means of enhancing their struggle and an advanced stage in the battle against colonialism, Zionism and exploitation—a battle which was led by progressive national forces and directed to achieve the aims of the Arab Nation: Unity, Freedom and Socialism.

In the Syrian Arab Region, after the achievement of independence, the masses of our people continued their struggle and were able, through a strenuous and intensified endeavour to achieve the great victory of launching the Revolution of the 8th of March 1963, under the leadership of the Baath Arab Socialist Party, which harnessed power to serve the endeavour to build up the united socialist Arab society.

The Baath Arab Socialist party was the first movement in the Arab Homeland to give Arab unity its true revolutionary meaning, to combine the national and the socialist struggles and to represent the will of the Arab Nation and its aspiration to a future, linking it with its glorious past and qualifying it to play an appropriate part in the victory of the cause of the liberation of all peoples.

In the course of the militant march of the party came the Corrective movement of the 16th of November 1970, in response to the needs and aspirations of our people. This movement represented an important specific development and a true embodiment of the spirit, principles and aims of the Party. It created the atmosphere favourable to the realization of a number of important achievements in the interests of the masses. First among these was the establishment of the Federation of the Arab Republics in response to the call for unity, a call which occupies a privileged place in the Arab conscience and which has been enhanced by the common Arab struggle against colonialism, Zionism and provincial and separatist trends and has been confirmed by the contemporary Arab revolution against domination and exploitation.

The above is the official English language translation of the Constitution as published by the Government of the Syrian Arab Republic.

Under the auspices of the Corrective movement an important step in the direction of consolidating the national unity of our masses has been accomplished. Led by the Baath Arab Socialist Party, a Progressive National Front has been established in a developed framework satisfying the needs and interests of the people and oriented to make of the masses, who are the instrument of the Arab revolution, a unified political organization.

The establishment of this constitution represents the crowning achievement of the struggle of our people to implement the principle of the adoption of a people's democracy, providing clear guidance to the future march of the people, a directive for the acts of the various establishments of the state and a source of its legislation.

This Constitution is based upon the following main principles:

1 — That the total Arab revolution represents a continuing and standing need to achieve the aims of the Arab Nation of Unity, Liberty and Socialism. The Revolution of the Syrian Arab Region is part of the total Arab revolution. Its policies in all fields derive from the general strategy of the Arab Revolution.

2 — All achievements which have been, or may be, attained by any Arab country in the present state of dismemberment are bound to be inadequate and incapable of reaching their full dimensions, as well as subject to deformation and setbacks unless enhanced and protected by Arab unity. Likewise, any danger from colonialism and Zionism menacing any Arab country is a danger that threatens the entire Arab Nation.

3 — The drive towards establishing a socialist regime in addition to its being a necessity emanating from the needs of Arab society, also represents a basic need to mobilize all the potentialities of the Arab masses in the battle against Zionism and Imperialism.

4 — Freedom is a sacred right, and a people's democracy is the ideal formula to guarantee for citizens the exercise of their freedom, which makes of them dignified human beings, capable of giving and achieving constructive work and of defending the homeland in which they live, and ready to offer sacrifices for the benefit of the nation to which they belong, inasmuch as the liberty of the homeland is only safeguarded by free citizens and the freedom of citizens is never complete unless they enjoy economic and social freedom.

5 — The Arab revolutionary movement is a basic part of the world liberation movement, and the struggle of the Arab people is part of the struggle of peoples who are fighting to achieve freedom, independence and progress.

This Constitution will serve as a guideline for the masses of our people spurring them to continue the battle of Liberation and Construction in the light of its principles and provisions, to consolidate their struggle and to hasten their steps towards the looked for future.

The following are excerpts from the Constitution's 156 articles:

PART ONE: Fundamental Principles
Chapter I: Political Principles

Article 1: 1 — The Syrian Arab Republic is a democratic people's state, sovereign and socialist. No part of its territory may be ceded. It is a member of the Federation of Arab Republics.

2 — The Syrian Arab Region is part of the Arab Homeland.

3 — The people of the Syrian Arab Region are part of the Arab Nation, who work and struggle to achieve all-embracing unity.

Article 3: 1 — Islam is the religion of the President of the Republic.

2 — Islamic Jurisprudence is a principal source of legislation.

Article 7: The constitutional oath of office shall be as follows: "I swear by Almighty God, loyally to safeguard the people's republican and democratic regime, to respect the laws and the Constitution, to watch over the interests of the people and the security of the Homeland, and to work and struggle to achieve the aim of the Arab Nation, of Unity, Liberty and Socialism."

Article 8: The Baath Arab Socialist Party shall be the leader party in society and the state and shall lead a National Progressive Front that works to unite the capacities of the masses of the people to serve the interests of the Arab Nation.

Chapter II—Economic Principles

Article 13: 1 — The economy of the state shall be socialist and planned and shall aim to abolish all forms of exploitation.

2 — Economic planning in Syria shall take into consideration the objective of realizing the economic integration of the Arab Homeland.

Article 14: The law shall organize property, which is of three kinds:

1 — People's property: This shall include natural resources, public services, and the establishments and institutions which are nationalized, or created, operated and supervised by the state in the interest of the people. These shall be protected by citizens.

2 — Collective property: This includes property owned by popular and professional organizations, by production units, cooperative societies and other social establishments. The law shall ensure protection and support for such property.

3 — Private property: includes property owned by individuals. The law shall define its social role in the service of national economy and within the development plan. Its manner of utilization shall not be directed against the interests of the people.

Chapter III—Principles of Education and Culture

Article 21: The educational and cultural system shall aim to bring up a national Arab generation, who are socialist and scientific in their manner of thinking, attached to their land and history, proud of their heritage, and imbued with the spirit of struggling to realize the aims of the nation of Unity, Liberty and Socialism, and of contributing to the service and progress of humanity.

Article 23: 1 — The national socialist culture shall be the basis of building up the unified socialist Arab society. It shall aim at enhancing moral values, realizing the ideals of the Arab Nation, developing society, and serving human causes; the state shall encourage and protect this culture.

3 — Physical education is a basic factor in building up society. It shall be encouraged by the state in order to bring up a generation, strong in body, character and thought.

Chapter IV: Freedom: Public Rights and Obligations

Article 25: 1 — Freedom is a sacred right. The state shall guarantee the personal freedom of citizens and safeguard their dignity and security.

Article 26: Every citizen shall have the right to participate in the political, economic, social and cultural life of the country. The law shall organize this participation.

. . . 3 — No one shall be subjected to physical or moral torture, or to treatment outrageous [to] dignity. The law shall define the penalties of such actions.

Article 35: . . . 2 — The state shall guarantee the performance of all religious rituals provided this does not violate public order.

Article 36: 1 — Work is the right and duty of every citizen. The state shall endeavour to ensure it for all citizens.

Article 40: 1 — All citizens shall be required to carry out the sacred duty of defending the security of the Homeland and of respecting the country's constitution and its unionist and socialist regime.

2 — Military service shall be compulsory and regulated by law.

Article 44: 1 — The family is the basic cell of society; it shall have the protection of the state.

Article 45: The state shall guarantee to women all opportunities enabling them to make complete and full contribution to the political, social, cultural and economic life of society. It shall endeavour to remove impediments that hinder their development and their participation in the building up of Arab socialist society.

PART FOUR

General and Transitional Provisions

Article 150: The Preamble to this Constitution shall be regarded as an integral and inseparable part of it.

TEXT OF AGREEMENT ON DISENGAGEMENT BETWEEN ISRAELI AND SYRIAN FORCES SIGNED 31 MAY, 1974

A. Israel and Syria will scrupulously observe the cease-fire on land, sea and air and will refrain from all military actions against each other, from the time of the signing of this document, in implementation of United Nations Security Council Resolution 338 dated 22 October, 1973.

B. The military forces of Israel and Syria will be separated in accordance with the following principles:

1. All Israeli military forces will be west of the line designated as Line A on the map attached hereto, except in the Quneitra area, where they will be west of Line A-1.

2. All territory east of Line A will be under Syrian administration, and Syrian civilians will return to this territory.

3. The area between Line A and the Line designated as Line B on the attached map will be an area of separation. In this area will be stationed the United Nations Disengagement Observer Force established in accordance with the accompanying protocol.

4. All Syrian military forces will be east of the line designated as Line B on the attached map.[1]

5. There will be two equal areas of limitation in armament and forces, one west of Line A and one east of Line B as agreed upon.

6. Air forces of the two sides will be permitted to operate up to their respective lines without interference from the other side.

C. In the area between Line A and Line A-1 on the attached map there shall be no military forces.

D. This agreement and the attached map will be signed by the military representatives of Israel and Syria in Geneva not later than 31 May, 1974, in the Egyptian-Israeli military working group of the Geneva Peace Conference under the aegis of the United Nations, after that group has been joined by a Syrian military representative, and with the participation of representatives of the United States and the Soviet Union. The precise delineation of a detailed map and a plan for the implementation of the disengagement of forces will be worked out by military representatives of Israel and Syria in the Egyptian-Israeli military working group who will agree on the stages of this process. The military working group described above will start their work for this purpose in Geneva under the aegis of the United Nations within 24 hours after the signing of this agreement. They will complete this task within five days. Disengagement will begin within 24 hours after the completion of the task of the military working group. The process of disengagement will be completed not later than twenty days after it begins.

---

1. See p. 166.

E. The provisions of paragraphs A, B and C shall be inspected by personnel of the United Nations comprising the United Nations Disengagement Observer Force under this agreement.

F. Within 24 hours after the signing of this agreement in Geneva all wounded prisoners of war which each side holds of the other as certified by the ICRC will be repatriated. The morning after the completion of the task of the military working group, all remaining prisoners of war will be repatriated.

G. The bodies of all dead soldiers held by either side will be returned for burial in their respective countries within 10 days after the signing of this agreement.

H. This agreement is not a peace agreement. It is a step toward a just and durable peace on the basis of Security Council Resolution 338 dated 22 October, 1973.

PROTOCOL TO AGREEMENT ON DISENGAGEMENT BETWEEN ISRAELI AND SYRIAN FORCES CONCERNING THE UNITED NATIONS DISENGAGEMENT OBSERVER FORCE

Israel and Syria agree that:

The function of the United Nations Disengagement Observer Force (UN-DOF) under the agreement will be to use its best efforts to maintain the cease-fire and to see that it is scrupulously observed. It will supervise the agreement and protocol thereto with regard to the areas of separation and limitation. In carrying out its mission, it will comply with generally applicable Syrian laws and regulations and will not hamper the functioning of local civil administration. It will enjoy freedom of movement and communication and other facilities that are necessary for its mission. It will be mobile and provided with personal weapons of a defensive character and shall use such weapons only in self-defense. The number of the UNDOF shall be about 1,250, who will be selected by the Secretary General of the United Nations in consultation with the parties from members of the United Nations who are not permanent members of the Security Council.

The UNDOF will be under the command of the United Nations, vested in the Secretary General, under the authority of the Security Council.

The UNDOF shall carry out inspections under the agreement, and report thereon to the parties, on a regular basis, not less often than once every fifteen days, and, in addition, when requested by either party. It shall mark on the site the respective lines shown on the map attached to the agreement.

Israel and Syria will support a resolution of the United Nations Security Council which will provide for the UNDOF contemplated by the agreement. The initial authorization will be for six months subject to renewal by further resolution of the Security Council.

Concerning Amnesty International's Report on Syrian and Israeli POWs of the War of October, 1973

Following accusations by Israel and Syria about maltreatment and torture of POWs by the other party during the war of 1973, a three-man Commission of Amnesty International visited Israel and Syria in October 1974 to investigate the allegations made by each party. The Commission's report was published in London by Amnesty International on April 10, 1975. The report confirmed the Israeli accusations and raised doubts regarding the Syrian accusations.

The Commission was criticized by Israel and by international authorities as failing to give Israel the opportunity to disprove the Syrian accusations. In a number of cases, Syrian accusations were not checked by consultation with the International Red Cross, which was possible, such as complaints by some Syrians who maintained that they did not receive visits by Red Cross representatives, and Syrian assertions that Israel did not submit reports on the medical condition of the Syrian POWs.

The report blamed both parties for failing to repatriate their respective POWs as soon as the hostilities had ended (as called for in the Geneva Convention) but did not state that, immediately after the end of the war, Israel repeatedly attempted to arrange an exchange of POWs while Syria refused to repatriate its Israeli POWs and withheld their names and serial numbers for five months. Israel objected to the fact that the Commission, which visited Israel before visiting Syria, had given only short notice of its arrival and that it was therefore very difficult for the Israeli authorities to foresee what accusations the Syrians were likely to make so that the necessary material could be gathered to disprove them. In those instances in which Israel anticipated the Syrian accusations and prepared refutations, the Commission accepted the Israeli medical reports on the treatment of the Syrian POWs.

In one case the Commission gave some support to a Syrian complaint by the schoolteacher, Yassir Hassan Rikab, who maintained that an Israeli guard had burnt him with cigarettes. The report stated that he carried marks which "resemble" cigarette burns.

The Commission found that Syria could not provide medical evidence to refute Israeli accusations. In the case of Gabi Gerson—a pilot who parachuted from his plane and landed safely, but who later lost one leg as a result of torture and medical neglect—Syria maintained that it had submitted X-rays and other medical data to the Red Cross when the POWs were repatriated.

According to the Commission, both parties maintained that they did not receive medical documents concerning the returned POWs. The report also stated: "The Syrian authorities—contrary to their claims—did not follow the procedure of returning medical reports together with the POWs," and that the Syrians had made many accusations but delivered no medical proof, although these were requested.

The Report pointed out that Syria had violated the Geneva Convention on the treatment of POWs by holding the Israeli POWs in a regular prison where they were exposed to brutality from the other prisoners.

Interviews with Israeli P.O.W.s

GABI GERSON

"I ran into ack-ack fire. The plane fell apart in midair. I managed to bail out the last minute. I parachuted down in an area full of Syrian soldiers. They got to the spot very quickly. Before they came near they began shooting at me from all directions. When I saw I had no chance of getting away—there were so many of them—I stopped, raised my hands and gave myself up. I tried not to make any suspicious moves. I tried not to make them nervous, else one of them might fire a burst by mistake. Their behavior was according to the rules. No beating, no prodding. Several senior Syrian officers in the area took over. They put me into a car and drove quickly to Damascus. There they took me straight to the first interrogation. It was pretty thorough, the way the Syrians interrogate.
What did they do to you?
I'd rather not go into details. I can't. Suffice to say, as a result of the interrogation I was taken to the hospital.
They took you to the hospital directly from the interrogation?
No. I was in perfect shape when we first came to Damascus. I landed well and nothing happened on the way from that spot to Damascus. In the course of the interrogation they shattered my left leg, below the knee. Nothing was left of it. Then they threw me into a solitary cell.
Why were you selected to appear on an interview over the French television?
I assume it's because I expressed opposition to the bombing of civilians. When the French asked the Syrians to allow them to interview an Israeli captive, they decided I was the suitable one. I had a specific reason for wanting this interview—to let it be known that I was alive. I knew my family would be overjoyed. The Syrians deleted the part where I told the French interviewer that I had gotten to Damascus in good physical condition. They also deleted the portions where I told how the Syrians treated us. Of course they retained the part where I said good things about the doctors. But they deserved it."

Ma'ariv, (Israel), June 7, 1974

BENYAMIN KIRYATI

He was hit while still in the plane, managed to parachute down and lost consciousness. His co-pilot was killed. He regained consciousness when he heard the sound of a Syrian helicopter. The Syrian soldiers in the helicopter fired at him, and he was hit by flying fragments of rock.
The Syrians took him to a hospital and operated on his cheek. Later he didn't receive any care at all—not antibiotics, nor change of bandages and no doctor's examinations. Two days after the operation he was removed to solitary confinement in a cellar cell.
"I took the sutures out by myself, with my fingernail. About twenty-five days later I had high fever and difficulty in breathing. I asked for medical help but was

refused. I was sure I would never leave the place alive. Fortunately my body overcame the illness.''

The interrogation began as soon as he was put into the cell. Each session was six hours long and was accompanied with beatings and torture. Since his eyes were bandaged, it was impossible to anticipate the blows.

''I was taken for interrogation to a separate room. The questioning was in Hebrew and English. I sat there, hands on knees, Behind me stood one of the jailers who kept striking me with a stick, as if to make his presence known. Whenever I answered, 'I don't know' or 'I don't remember'—down came the stick. Then the interrogation would go on with my eyes open and a glaring light thrust close to them. They also used lamps to sear the skin. Worst of all were the beatings with a thin stick across the bottom of the feet.''

In his cell Beni had a pitcher of water and two blankets—later four—and was allowed to go to the lavatory three times in 24 hours. On the way there, he was beaten by any of the guards he encountered. Even in his cell he was beaten every now and then by the jailers, for no reason at all. His ''meals'' consisted of bread and one or two olives, plus a drop of jelly and a triangle of cheese for breakfast and supper, and a slice of bread with barley cereal and at times a piece of suet at noon.

For two days the pilot lay in his dirty, blood-encrusted bed. On the third day he was given clean pyjamas for a television appearance, but under it his body was still caked with blood. Ten days later he was allowed to bathe, prior to an interview with a Lebanese reporter. The next time he had a bath was just before his release.

''They asked me if I thought it was necessary to bomb children's homes or hospitals. I told them I was opposed to it, but the paper presented me as having been on just such a bombing mission. I did try to keep the interview on a tone that would ease the pressure on me.''

The worst of all were the terrible cries of the tortured in the cellar. These went on around the clock. During his entire imprisonment, Beni spent only three days outside his cell.

At no time during his imprisonment was Beni visited by a member of the Red Cross. A package and two letters sent to him by his parents were handed to him one day before his release.

Ma'ariv, (Israel), June 7, 1974

Syria rejected the accusations made by returned Israel captives regarding their torture while in prison. Radio Damascus declared: ''Syria will no longer deal fairly with the captives it will take, should Israel continue torturing the captives it takes.''

A Syrian radio commentator said: ''Israel must remember that the war is not over. There is no difficulty in taking Israel hostages or prisoners, and Israel should therefore switch from a policy of terror toward the prisoners, otherwise Syria will cease treating the prisoners it holds with dignity.''

Davar, (Israel), June 9, 1974

Text of Letters to the U.N. Secretary-General from Syria and Israel Regarding Quneitra

Letter dated 30 July 1974 from the Permanent Representative of the Syrian Arab Republic to the United Nations addressed to the Secretary-General

Upon instruction from my Government, I have the honour to draw your attention to the fact that during the implementation of the Agreement on Disengagement between Israeli and Syrian Forces signed in Geneva on 31 May 1974, upon the withdrawal from the occupied Syrian territory, the Israeli forces perpetrated crimes of destruction of Syrian civilian villages, especially the destruction of the city of Quneitra, using for this aim explosives and bulldozers.

These Israeli acts constitute a flagrant violation of international law, humanitarian principles and civilized values, as well as a clear violation of the Geneva Convention of 12 August 1949 relative to the Protection of Civilian Persons in Time of War,[1] especially since these acts have been perpetrated without any reason. Article 53 of the above-mentioned Convention provides that:

"Any destruction by the Occupying Power of real or personal property belonging individually or collectively to private persons, or to the State, or to other public authorities, or to social or co-operative organizations, is prohibited, except where such destruction is rendered absolutely necessary by military operations."

Moreover, international law has considered such acts committed by Israel as war crimes. Article 6 (b) of the Charter of the International Military Tribunal of Nuremberg[2] considered as war crimes the wanton destruction of cities, towns and villages not justified by military necessity.

I would therefore be grateful if your Excellency could provide the necessary steps and arrangements in order to verify on the spot these Israeli acts and to disseminate the results of the verification.

I should be grateful if you would have the text of this letter circulated as an official document of the General Assembly and the Security Council.

(Signed) Haissam KELANI
Ambassador
Permanent Representative of the
Syrian Arab Republic to the
United Nations

1. United Nations, Treaty Series, vol. 75, No. 973, p. 287.
2. Ibid., vol. 82, No. 251, p. 284.

74-20027

A/9568-S/11396, 30 July 1974.

Letter dated 2 August 1974 from the Permanent Representative of Israel to the United Nations addressed to the Secretary-General

On instructions of my Government, I have the honour to refer to the letter addressed to you on 30 July 1974 (A/9568-S/11396) by the Permanent Representative of Syria and to state the following:

> It is a matter of common knowledge that the damage and destruction caused in front-line villages and in the town of Quneitra are the direct result of acts of aggression carried out by Syria in various periods since 1967, culminating in its war of aggression against Israel in October 1973 and accompanied by Syria's persistent rejection of all peace-making efforts, including its refusal for many years to accept Security Council Resolution 242 (1967).

> The claim that the town of Quneitra was allegedly destroyed in one deliberate Israeli action, on the eve of its evacuation by the Israeli forces, is nothing but a crude propaganda fabrication. This is not the first time that the Syrian Government has tried to conceal its guilt by blaming others for situations of its own making.

I have the honour to request that this letter be circulated as an official document of the General Assembly and the Security Council.

> *(Signed)* Yosef TEKOAH
> Permanent Representative of Israel
> to the United Nations

74-20502   A/9570-S/11408, 2 August 1974.

Letter dated 12 September 1974 from the Permanent Representative of the Syrian Arab Republic to the United Nations addressed to the Secretary-General

On instructions from my Government, and further to my previous letters concerning the incessant acts of aggression perpetrated by Israel against Syria in violation of humanitarian and international principles and of the Convention for the Protection of Cultural Property in the Event of Armed Conflict,[1] done at the Hague on 14 May 1954, and ratified by Israel as well as by Syria, I have the honour to transmit to you herewith a preliminary report by the Directorate General of Antiquities and Museums, concerning the violation by the Israeli occupation authorities of the principles of international law by the destruction and pillaging of archaeological sites and historical monuments in the liberated area in Syria and the acts of barbarism committed by Israel during its occupation of the Golan region and the city of Quneitra:

> "The Directorate General of Antiquities and Museums instructed a commission of archaeological experts to inspect the archaeological sites

and historical monuments in the area liberated from the Israeli occupation forces and to record the damage caused to such sites and monuments. The team visited the entire area several times, with the exception of a few places which are still mined or to which access is difficult.

"The first place to be visited was the city of Quneitra, the district capital. This is an ancient city, the old quarters of which have a special character and contain several monuments listed in the registers of the Directorate General of Antiquities and Museums (mosques, churches, schools . . .).

"The Israeli occupation forces did not spare these quarters and monuments from deliberate destruction one or two days before the evacuation. The traces of explosions and fire were still fresh.

"With regard to other sites, the commission found that the Israelis had completely ruined certain sites, such as Tel Merei, and had carried off many architectural features from historical monuments (stones, capitals, lintels, etc.): for example, a lintel was taken from the home of Mr. Tarif Hamadé at Kafer Nasej and several carved stones were taken from the home of Mr. Ghaleb Yassin Moustapha at Mashara. In addition, the Israelis took measures to remove and carry off a large number of architectural features marked and numbered in red."

Thus, the Israeli authorities destroyed and pillaged the cultural property in the Golan area and also completely destroyed the city of Quneitra and the village of Rafid, including the cultural, religious and historical buildings as well as the schools. These acts constitute a violation of article 1 of the Hague Convention, which defines cultural property as follows:

"(a) movable or immovable property of great importance to the cultural heritage of every people, such as monuments of architecture, art or history, whether religious or secular; archaeological sites; groups of buildings which, as a whole, are of historical or artistic interest; as well as scientific collections and important collections of books or archives or of reproductions of the property defined above;

"(b) buildings whose main and effective purpose is to preserve or exhibit the movable cultural property defined in subparagraph (a) such as museums, large libraries and depositories of archives, and refuges intended to shelter, in the event of armed conflict, the movable cultural property defined in subparagraph (a)."

By its failure to respect cultural property, Israel violated article 4 of the Convention, paragraphs 1 and 3 of which state:

"1. The High Contracting Parties undertake to respect cultural property situated within their own territory as well as within the territory of other High Contracting Parties by refraining from any use of the property and its immediate surroundings or of the appliances in use for its protection for purposes which are likely to expose it to destruction or damage in the event of armed conflict; and by refraining from any act of hostility directed against such property.

"3. The High Contracting Parties further undertake to prohibit, prevent and, if necessary, put a stop to any form of theft, pillage or misappropriation of, and any acts of vandalism directed against, cultural property. They shall refrain from requisitioning movable cultural property situated in the territory of another High Contracting Party."

Israel committed an act of barbarism without parallel in history by taking criminal measures against all the cultural property of Quneitra, Rafid and the Golan area, ignoring article 4, paragraph 4, of the Convention, which states:

"4. They [the High Contracting Parties] shall refrain from any act directed by way of reprisals against cultural property."

Thus, Israel took not a single step to safeguard the cultural property in the area it occupied, but, on the contrary, completely destroyed it in violation of article 5, paragraphs 1 and 2, of the Convention, which state:

"1. Any High Contracting Party in occupation of the whole or part of the territory of another High Contracting Party shall as far as possible support the competent national authorities of the occupied territory in safeguarding and preserving its cultural property.

"2. Should it prove necessary to take measures to preserve cultural property situated in occupied territory and damaged by military operations, and should the competent national authorities be unable to take such measures, the Occupying Power shall, as far as possible, and in close co-operation with such authorities, take the most necessary measures of preservation."

I should be grateful if you would arrange to have the text of this letter circulated as an official document of the General Assembly and the Security Council and transmit it to the Commission on Human Rights and the Special Committee to Investigate Israeli Practices Affecting the Human Rights of the Population of the Occupied Territories.

(Signed) Haissam KELANI
Ambassador
Permanent Representative of the
Syrian Arab Republic to the
United Nations

74-24059

A/9683-S/11506, 12 September, 1974.

Letter dated 23 September 1974 from the Permanent Representative of Israel to the United Nations addressed to the Secretary-General

On instructions of my Government, I have the honour to refer to the letter addressed to you by the Permanent Representative of the Syrian Arab Republic on 12 September 1974 (A/9683-S/11506).

The Syrian letter is the usual propaganda attempt to divert attention, by means of repeated distortion and falsification, from Syria's reprehensible international conduct. The allegations contained in the above-mentioned letter have already been refuted. In my letter to you of 2 August 1974 (A/9570-S/11408), I pointed out that the damage and destruction caused in front-line villages, in the town of Quneitra and in their vicinity are the direct result of acts of aggression carried out by Syria in various periods since 1967 culminating in its war of aggression in October 1973 and continued in Syria's systematic violations of the cease-fire following that war.

Though the method of trying to shift to others responsibility for its own destructive actions is not new in Syria's case, it is, however, bizarre that the Syrian Government should apply this method with a persistence that puts in doubt the credibility of all its claims and complaints.

Its alleged concern for the damage caused by war to cultural sites is particularly hollow in view of its indiscriminate attacks on peaceful Israeli villages and the destruction of innumerable articles of religious value perpetrated on Yom Kippur, the holiest of days to the Jewish people, sacred to and respected also by all mankind.

Thus Syria, which initiated the war and continued its artillery bombardment even after the Security Council cease-fire resolution, bears full responsibility for the destruction resulting therefrom.

It is to be observed that Israel is a signatory to the Hague Convention for the Protection of Cultural Property in the Event of Armed Conflict of 14 May 1954[1] and acts in conformity with it.

The statements transmitted to you on 12 September 1974 by the Permanent Representative of Lebanon (A/9684-S/11507) and on 13 September 1974 by the Permanent Representative of Algeria (S/11508) repeat Syria's baseless charges and are obviously a vain attempt to give them at least verbal support.

I have the honour to request that this letter be circulated as an official document of the General Assembly and the Security Council.

> (*Signed*) Yosef TEKOAH
> Permanent Representative of Israel
> to the United Nations

1. United Nations *Treaty Series*, vol. 249, p. 240, No. 3511.
1. United Nations, *Treaty Series*, vol. 249, No. 3511.

Excerpts from a Statement by the Pan-Arab Command of the Ba'th Arab Socialist Party on the Occasion of the Second Anniversary of the War of October, 1973

The October War was a field test of our nation's legacy and heritage after the June 1967 setback, which Zionism and Imperialism designed to frustrate our nation's revolutionary spirit. But in the October War of Liberation our nation has succeeded in resurrecting "enlivening" all the sources of struggle and perseverence our nation possesses; and in absorbing the blow, and starting preparations and massing for a new confrontation that constituted the first Arab clash in terms of decision making, planning and execution.

Whatever victories our nation has scored as a result of the October War are the harvest of only very little of the capacities and capabilities which were massed and gathered in the War of Liberation—which intuitively indicates that our nation is able—with its great and vast capabilities—to achieve, if these are used in the coming and inevitable confrontation with the enemy, to achieve a decisive victory that will force the enemy to yield to the Arab nation's demands at this stage, represented in a total withdrawal of the enemy troops from all Arab occupied territories, and in recognizing the national rights of the people of Palestine.

The Egyptian-Israeli agreement has diverted the Arab-Israeli conflict away from its major facts, and transformed its original dimensions as a conflict for "survival" between Arab nationalism and its growing liberation movement, and world Zionism as aggressive invading ideology and policy, into one of marginal differences over border issues that can be solved through dialogues and co-existence, ignoring the essence of the Zionist settler nature based on imposing on the Arabs a homogenous imported existence forcibly transplanted as a fait-accompli in our homeland.

This retreat on the Arab side has created parallel gains on the Zionist side that surpassed and certainly went beyond all the dreams of Zionism built on the June 1967 aggression. These Zionist goals were rejected by the Arabs, first and foremost by Egypt—from a position of military and political defeat—while they are being accepted now by the Egyptian Regime from a position of victory after the October War!!

When the Ba'th Arab Socialist Party condemns the Egyptian-Israeli agreement and rejects any partial solution to the issue as well as partitioning that issue itself—the party does in fact reassert its commitments and Pan-Arab responsibilities.

The battle with the Zionist enemy is continuing on all levels as long as the Zionist enemy still occupies a foothold of our Arab Land.

As reported in *Flash of Damascus*, No. 48, November 1975.

182

Excerpts of a Speech by President Hafez Al-Assad on the Second Anniversary of the War of October, 1973

"We cannot say, as some have already said, that what is related to Syria should be decided by the Syrians. What is related to our struggle against 'Israel' is not merely a matter of consultation, but it is a decision to be taken and carried out. It is above any other regional decisions. There is no place for regional issues whatsoever in our struggle against the enemy."

"Syria knows and is aware of its enemies, it fought bravely and with great honor. The Syrian Forces stormed one of the most intricate defensive lines ever known in military history without taking the enemy on surprise. The report of the Agranat Committee proved that the attack on the western front had been a complete surprise to 'Israel.' But our attack in the Northern front was expected as the enemy had already mobilized all its forces to the Golan Heights as a captive."

"The enemy retaliated by bombing Damascus, which bravely withstood the raids. Israeli planes and pilots fell one after the other in Damascus and its suburbs. They bombed too Homs, Tartous, Lattakia, and many other towns and villages and civilian targets."

"If there are to be talks for new momentum on the Syrian front, they must be accompanied by similar action on the Palestine front through the Palestine Liberation Organization."

"Israel is trying to smudge the Palestine case, and it has not recognized Palestinian rights. Palestinian Arabs were concerned because of current Arab attitude, particularly after the Sinai agreement."

(On the Egyptian-Israeli agreement, President Assad said:)

"We ask the Americans, who made this agreement, whether in the event of a war with the Soviet Union and the occupation of their land they would agree to the passage of Soviet goods through their territory."

"We differ completely with our brothers in Egypt over the Sinai agreement and are opposed to it for many reasons. It constitutes a departure from Arab solidarity and unanimity, and from the resolutions of the Summit conferences at Rabat and Algiers."

"This agreement has led to immobilizing the Egyptian front and embodied a major tragedy in its secret clauses."

"Our brothers in Egypt had denied more than once the existence of secret documents. Then the American Congress officially proclaimed the existence of these documents and disclosed some of them."

(Criticizing the deployment of American experts at the early warning centers, President Assad said the U.S. was not neutral, and even if it had been "would it be possible for Egypt to give up its right to sovereignty over its territory?")

"The agreement was not for limited duration, contrary to what had been said in Cairo."

"The agreement allows Israeli goods to pass through an Arab Canal while 'Israel' occupies all Palestine, whose people were driven out. The same was done in Golan, Jerusalem and Sinai."

(President Assad added that "there was the lately revealed confidential documents which made one wonder how the Egyptian authority accepted them.")

(President Assad added that the agreement carried a lot of implications. The first and foremost of these was the "discord among Arab ranks. It is the strategy of the enemy.")

(Another was to isolate the Palestine issue.) "They want us here in Syria to start talks that lead to unilateral action and in turn lead to isolating the Palestine issue. Thus, they spread the rumor that Syria is on the way to another disengagement of forces. We believe that our cause is one, and that the Palestinian issue is the mother issue. We will never allow the Israeli strategy to succeed in isolating it, because it is our issue, for which we fought in the past and in October. Around this issue turns our struggle in this region and the struggle of all the Arab nation."

(The second implication was its Political aspect. President Assad believes that, unlike the previous disengagement of forces, the present agreement was all political.)

"The people of Palestine," the President went on to say, " are not in need of tactful talk. What they truly need is sincere, true and serious action. We imagine that the Palestinians, especially those who are subjected to Israeli occupation, are deeply worried due to (the) present Arab situation resulting from the Sinai agreement; but I am sure that this anxiety will never develop into a state of despair . . . because the whole Arab nation stands by their side."

(President Assad concluded his speech by sending his regards to the Palestinian Arab citizens under occupation, and assured them that Arab struggle and willingness are endless.)

As reported in *Flash of Damascus*, No. 48, November 1975. President Assad delivered the above address at a meeting at the University of Damascus.

Sources

Antonious, George. *The Arab Awakening*. New York: Capricorn Books, 1965.

Area Handbook for Syria, 2nd Edition. Published 1971. USGPO: Washington, D.C.

Bar-Yaacov, Natan. *The Israel-Syrian Armistice, Problems of Implementation 1949-1966.* Jerusalem: The Magnes Press, the Hebrew University, 1967.

Dawisha, A. I. "The Transnational Party in Regional Politics: The Arab Ba'th Party." *Asian Affairs Journal,* Vol. 61 (New Series, Vol. V) Part 1, Februrary, 1974.

Fisher, W. B. "Syria, Physical and Social Geography." *The Middle East and North Africa* (1974-75) Europa Publications Ltd., Twenty-First Edition.

Haim, Sylvia G. "The Ba'ath in Syria," in Curtis, Michael, ed. *People and Politics in the Middle East.* New Brunswick, N.J.: Transaction Press, 1971. Published under the auspices of the American Academic Association for Peace in the Middle East.

Hourani, A. H. *Syria and Lebanon: A Political Essay.* Issued under the auspices of the Royal Institute of International Affairs. London, New York, Toronto: Oxford University Press, 1971.

Howard, Harry N. *An American Inquiry in the Middle East, The King-Crane Commission.* Beirut: Khayat, 1963.

Khadduri, Majid. "The Scheme of Fertile Crescent Unity: A Study in Inter-Arab Relations," in Frye, Richard N. ed. *The Near East and the Great Powers.* Port Washington, New York: Kennikat Press, Inc., 1969.

Levine, Evyatar, and Shimoni, Yaacov. Editors. *Political Dictionary of the Middle East in the 20th Century.* Revised Edition. New York: Quadrangle, 1974.

Lewis, Bernard. "The Return of Islam." *Commentary.* Vol. 61, No. 1. January 1976.

Ma'oz, Moshe. "Syria Under Hafiz al-Asad: New Domestic and Foreign Policies." *Jerusalem Papers on Peace Problems,* No. 15, The Leonard Davis Institute for International Relations, The Hebrew University of Jerusalem, Israel. 1975.

Porath, Y. *The Emergence of the Palestinian-Arab National Movement, 1918-1929.* London: Frank Cass, 1974.

Rabinovich, Itamar. *Syria Under the Ba'th 1963-66: The Army-Party Symbiosis.* New York: Halsted Press, 1972.

Safran, Nadav. *From War to War.* New York: Pegasus, 1969.

Seal, Patrick. *The Struggle for Syria: A Study of Post-War Arab Politics 1945-1958.* Issued under the auspices of the Royal Institute of International Affairs. London: New York, Toronto: Oxford University Press, 1965.

Syria, "Published on Occasion of the Diversion of the Euphrates, 5th July, 1973." Office Arabe de Presse et de Documentation (OFA), Damascus.

Additional Reading

Abboushi, W. F. *Political Systems of the Middle East in the 20th Century.* New York: Dodd Mead & Co., 1970.

Abu Jaber, Kamel S. *The Arab Ba'th Socialist Party: History, Ideology and Organization.* Syracuse, New York. 1966.

Agwani, M. S. "The Ba'th: A Study in Contemporary Arab Politics." *International Studies,* III (1961).

Arberry, A. J. General Editor. *Religion in the Middle East.* 2 vols. London: Cambridge University Press. 1969.

Ashkar, Riad. "The Syrian & Egyptian Campaigns." *Journal of Palestine Studies,* Vol. III, No. 2, Winter 1974. Published jointly by the Institute for Palestine Studies & Kuwait University in Beirut, Lebanon.

Avineri, Shlomo. "Modernization and Arab Society: Some Reflections." *Israel, the Arabs and the Middle East.* Edited by Irving Howe and Carl Gershman. New York: Basic Books, 1972.

Baer, G. *Population and Society in the Arab East.* New York: Praeger, 1964.

Be'eri, E. *Army Officers in Arab Politics and Society.* New York and London: Praeger, 1970.

Ben-Tsur, A. "The Neo-Ba'th Party of Syria." *Journal of Contemporary History,* III, 1968.

Binder, L. *The Ideological Revolution in the Middle East.* New York: John Wiley & Sons, 1964.

————. "The Tragedy of Syria." *World Politics,* XIX, 1967.

Dabbagh, S. M. "Agrarian Reform in Syria." *Middle East Economic Papers,* 1962.

Dann, U. *Iraq Under Qassem: A Political History, 1958-1963.* New York: Praeger, 1969.

Dawn, C. E. "The Question of Nationalism in Syria and Lebanon." in W. Sands (ed.) *Tensions in the Middle East.* Washington, D.C.: Middle East Institute, 1956.

————. "From Ottomanism to Arabism: The Origin of an Ideology." *Review of Politics,* XXIII. 1961.

Garzouzi, E. "Land Reform in Syria." *Middle East Journal,* XVII. 1963.

Grunebaum, G. E. von. *Modern Islam.* New York: Vintage Books, 1964.

Haim, Sylvia. *Arab Nationalism: An Anthology.* Berkeley and Los Angeles: University of California Press, 1964.

Halpern, M. *The Politics of Social Change in the Middle East and North Africa.* New Jersey: Princeton University Press, 1963.

Hansen, B. *Economic Development in Syria*. Santa Monica, Calif.: Rand Corporation, 1969.

Holt, P. M., Lambton, Ann K. S., Lewis, Bernard. Editors. *The Cambridge History of Islam*. 2 vols. London: Cambridge University Press. 1970.

Hottinger, A. "Syria: War Psychosis as an Instrument of Government." *Swiss Review of World Affairs*, XVII. 1967.

———. "How the Arab Bourgeoisie Lost Power." *Journal of Contemporary History*, III. 1968.

Hourani, A. H. *Minorities in the Arab World*. London: Oxford University Press, 1964.

Hurewitz, J. C. *Middle East Politics: The Military Dimension*. New York: Octagon Books, 1974.

Khadduri, M. *Political Trends in the Arab World: The Role of Ideas and Ideals in Politics*. Baltimore: Johns Hopkins Press, 1970.

Landes, David S. "Palestine Before the Zionists." *Commentary*, Vol. 61, No. 2, February 1976.

Lenczowski, G. "Radical Regimes in Egypt, Syria and Iraq: Some Comparative Observations in Ideologies and Practices." *Journal of Politics*, XXVII. 1966.

Lerner, D. *The Passing of Traditional Society*. New York: The Free Press, 1964.

Lipset, S. M. "The Dynamics of Power in Syria Since the Break with Egypt." *Middle Eastern Studies*, VI. 1970.

Ma'oz, Moshe. "Syria Under Hafiz al-Asad: New Domestic and Foreign Policies." *Jerusalem Papers on Peace Problems*, No. 15, The Leonard Davis Institute for International Relations, The Hebrew University of Jerusalem, Israel. 1975.

Silberman, Gad. *Revolution and Arab Socialism*. Published by the Israel Academic Committee on the Middle East, Jerusalem. March 1973.

Stein, Leonard. *The Balfour Declaration*. London: Valentine, Mitchell & Co., Ltd., 1961.

Tibawi, A. L. *A Modern History of Syria, Including Lebanon and Palestine*. London: MacMillan, 1969.

Torrey, Gordon H. "Aspects of the Political Elite in Syria." *Political Elites in the Middle East*. Edited by George Lenczowski. Washington, D.C.: The American Enterprise Institute for Public Policy Research, 1975.

Ziadeh, N. *Syria and Lebanon*. New York: Praeger, 1957.

Index